The Future of Hedge Fund Investing

Founded in 1807, John Wiley & Sons is the oldest independent publishing company in the United States. With offices in North America, Europe, Australia, and Asia, Wiley is globally committed to developing and marketing print and electronic products and services for our customers' professional and personal knowledge and understanding.

The Wiley Finance series contains books written specifically for finance and investment professionals as well as sophisticated individual investors and their financial advisors. Book topics range from portfolio management to e-commerce, risk management, financial engineering, valuation and financial instrument analysis, as well as much more.

For a list of available titles, please visit our Web site at www.Wiley Finance.com.

The Future of Hedge Fund Investing

A Regulatory and Structural Solution for a Fallen Industry

MONTY AGARWAL

WILEY

John Wiley & Sons, Inc.

Published by John Wiley & Sons, Inc., Hoboken, New Jersey.
Published simultaneously in Canada.

For general information on our other products and services or for technical support, please contact our Customer Care Department within the United States at (800) 762-2974, outside the United States at (317) 572-3993 or fax (317) 572-4002.

Wiley also publishes its books in a variety of electronic formats. Some content that appears in print may not be available in electronic books. For more information about Wiley products, visit our website at www.wiley.com.

Library of Congress Cataloging-in-Publication Data:
Agarwal, Monty, 1968–
  The future of hedge fund investing : a regulatory and structural solution for a fallen industry/ Monty Agarwal.
      p. cm. – (Wiley finance series)
  Includes bibliographical references and index.
  ISBN 978-0-470-53744-2 (cloth)
      1. Hedge funds.   I. Title.
  HG4530.A38 2009
  332.64′524–dc22

                                                                      2009023576

Printed in the United States of America

10 9 8 7 6 5 4 3 2 1

Dedicated to my children, Kieran and Meghan.

May they grow up to become wise investors.

Contents

Foreword

Hedge funds employ some of the brightest minds in the fields of finance, mathematics, and the sciences. But that did absolutely nothing to help save investors from Bernie Madoff's $65 billion Ponzi scheme, the largest swindle in the history of mankind. Nor did it protect them from recent 50 percent-plus losses at some of the largest and most established hedge funds in the world.

What happened? Where was the Securities and Exchange Commission (SEC)? Should investors forget about hedge funds entirely and go back to buying and holding simple stock indexes, bland mutual funds, or 2 percent certificates of deposit (CDs)?

This book provides the answers: The scandals and dismal performance of the immediate past can be turned into a great opportunity for the immediate future.

First and foremost, it's an opportunity to *learn* the best of lessons that can only be taught by the greatest of shocks. Investors can learn how to better identify the early warning signs of bad intent or bad performance. Plus, regulators can learn more precisely how to restore and maintain investor confidence.

The hedge fund industry as a whole is not on the precipice of perversity, and every hedge fund manager is not on the edge of evil. Quite to the contrary, provided investors can learn how to better select the right ones, they can reap the advantages of:

- *True diversification across multiple asset classes.* Hedge funds invest not only in stocks and bonds, but also in currencies, commodities, and real estate.
- *True global diversification.* Average investors seeking to expand beyond U.S. borders can buy exchange-traded funds (ETFs) linked to major foreign markets or a limited universe of foreign stocks traded on U.S. exchanges. Through hedge funds, however, they can access a far broader range of overseas investment opportunities.
- *Noncorrelation with traditional investments.* The devastating losses in 2008 demonstrate that even the best diversification can be for naught when nearly all investments fall in unison. However, as their name implies, hedge funds were originally designed to hedge against that risk, deploying investment strategies that actually profit from market adversity.

- *Performance!* Yes, unfortunately, many hedge funds went along with the crowd and lost just as much money as—or more than—ordinary, buy-and-hold stock investors. Fortunately, however, the exceptions do *not* prove that rule. You can still find exceptional fund managers producing stupendous—and legitimate—investment returns for their investors. Steve Cohen of SAC Capital and Jim Simmons of Renaissance Technologies, for example, have delivered 30 percent annualized returns for over 15 years running.

And they're not alone! There are currently over 7,000 hedge funds, which at their peak managed nearly $2 trillion. And today, quite a few are bound to achieve consistently high performance.

How? Just to give you one example, a growing group of hedge funds are now shifting their sights to major emerging markets, where even average retail investors buying ordinary ETFs have seen returns of 40 percent in China and 65 percent in Brazil—all in just in the first six months of 2009. And they did so even without leverage and without sophisticated trading strategies that hedge funds can deploy to not only help achieve high returns but also smooth out the dips in between.

Needless to say, high returns are not risk free. Nor can they be sustained indefinitely in all market conditions. But with an enhanced ability to choose the right hedge funds that this book provides, the opportunity for high, mostly consistent returns is undeniable.

Are hedge funds exclusively for large institutions and the superrich? Not anymore! With the advent of *funds of hedge funds*, the barriers to entry have been greatly reduced. Like mutual funds, these can do the heavy lifting for those who cannot: selecting the right funds . . . monitoring their performance . . . investing in the best and dumping the rest.

The fact that many funds of hedge funds have recently *failed* in this task does not mean they will fail in the future. Indeed, what makes this book so unique is that it draws the road map for success—not only for the funds' managers, but also for their investors.

Monty Agarwal covers the nuts and bolts of how investors in hedge funds currently make their investment decisions and build their portfolios. He diagnoses the ailments and provides a prescription for the cure.

Amid a sea of get-rich-quick schemes that too often distract investors from their mission, this book, by a seasoned veteran of the hedge fund industry, is exactly the kind of informed guide you want by your side.

Martin D. Weiss, PhD
President, Weiss Research, Inc.
Author of the current *New York Times* best seller,
The Ultimate Depression Survival Guide

Introduction

O ver the past 10 years I have been directly involved with the hedge fund industry, first running my own hedge fund, Predator Capital, and then working at other hedge funds. I saw firsthand the boom years of the hedge fund industry from 2003 to 2007 and the big bust of 2008. As I ran my own hedge fund, I conducted several meetings with investors, some high net worth investors but mostly funds of hedge funds, and was able to look at their due diligence process firsthand. I also realized that the funds of funds are an extremely important conduit in the flow of money from the end investors to the hedge fund managers. The end investors rely very heavily on the expertise of the funds of funds in selecting hedge fund managers who can best provide the investment returns. It did not take me long to realize that neither the high net worth investor nor the funds of funds have the necessary skilled professionals who can understand and therefore perform the necessary due diligence to manage hedge fund investments. In fact, a lot of the scams could have been detected at a much earlier stage if the hedge fund investors had the necessary skills.

My sincere hope is that anybody who has invested in hedge funds, is planning on investing in hedge funds, or is just plain curious about traders and hedge funds, will read this book. This book is an insider's critical look at the hedge fund industry. I am not writing this book to extol on the genius of the hedge fund industry or its mavens. There are no interviews with the top hedge fund managers or an insight into their secretive financial arsenals; there are several books already on these subjects. This book tries to explain the trading world of Wall Street and the makeup of its denizens such that the layman can understand what lies behind the gilded doors of a hedge fund. Along the way the book offers insight, not just for the institutional investor but also for the high net worth individual, into the advantages of investing in hedge funds, the pitfalls, and, more important, ways to avoid such pitfalls. Hedge funds are not a fad and will not disappear. The hedge fund industry generates liquidity and thereby improves the efficiency and functioning of the global capital markets. The investment community relies on the hedge fund industry to generate investment returns that feed the pension funds, university endowments, and the charitable foundations around the world. The industry deserves to be understood and therefore run better.

Unfortunately, there have been several instances where investors have invested into hedge funds with little or no due diligence, relying entirely on hearsay, reputation of the manager, or even worse, the manic desire to belong to an exclusive club. When due diligence is actually performed on a hedge fund manager, it is concentrated on checking the manager's background to uncover any legal or regulatory actions and operational due diligence to ensure that the hedge fund is properly set up with reputable auditors, brokers, and administrators. This level of due diligence ensures that the hedge fund manager is not a crook and will not run away with the investors' capital. While the operational due diligence is very important, it ranks a distant second to strategy-level due diligence, which for all intents and purposes is not being conducted effectively by the hedge fund investors, retail or institutional. It is the strategy-level due diligence that will ensure that hedge fund collapses such as Amaranth Advisors, Vega Asset Management, or Long Term Capital Management do not wipe out investors' capital either. More hedge fund investors have incurred massive losses on their investments due to a breakdown of trader discipline than to outright fraud. Ongoing strategy-level due diligence performed correctly would have prevented those cases and would have spotted charlatans like Bernie Madoff as well. This book is dedicated to defining a new framework for conducting strategy-level due diligence on hedges fund, which I believe does not exist in the industry at present.

To further address the dire need for appropriate hedge fund due diligence, I also launched a hedge fund consulting business called, MACM Hedge Fund Consulting. MACM Hedge Fund Consulting provides strategy and risk management consulting services to the hedge fund investor community, including high net worth investors, family offices, pension funds, endowments, sovereign wealth funds, and funds of funds. MACM is served by professionals who have extensive hands-on experience as proprietary traders and have traded capital, managed traders, and have a firm grasp of risk management principles and derivative instruments. The consultants at MACM have traded the strategies deployed at hedge funds, are aware of the risks involved as well as the ploys of the unscrupulous manager, which would not be evident to the untrained eye. The hedge fund investor community stands to benefit from our experience and insight. For further information on our customized, complete, and cost-effective solutions for all your hedge fund investing needs, please visit the website, www.macmllc .com, or contact me directly at magarwal@macmllc.com.

In January 2009, I decided to write a short article for magazine publication to share my views with the industry professionals. The article led me to write this book explaining in further detail the broken model and proposing a fix. The article I wrote in January 2009 is presented below and is a synopsis of the book.

FUNDS OF HEDGE FUNDS: TIME FOR CHANGE IS NOW

A fund of hedge funds, as the name suggests, invests not in any underlying security but in a portfolio of hedge funds in order to minimize idiosyncratic risk. If you quiz the management team of a fund of funds on their investment process, you will hear very eloquently designed phrases, such as top-down, bottom-up approach; combination of qualitative and quantitative analyses; fluid and dynamic processes; etc. While such scholarly phrases sound very impressive, they mask the truth that most funds of funds do not have the necessary skills to truly understand the trading strategies that they are invested in.

I witnessed the growth of the fund of funds industry while I was working at Bankers Trust, a pioneer in the fund of funds business. The approach to investing in hedge funds was and still is a backward-looking data-mining approach. A typical fund of funds will have monthly performance data of a hedge fund and will run statistical analysis on that data. It will apply efficient portfolio construction principles and pick a portfolio of hedge funds that have the highest returns with the lowest volatility. Because most fund of funds use the same statistics packages and portfolio construction principles, they all seem to come up with similar group of hedge funds to invest in.

Now that we know how a fund of funds invests and operates, it is no surprise that the investment committees at the funds of funds comprise people who have extensive experience in statistical analysis, traditional asset management, relationship banking, marketing, legal, and other fine professions. And herein lies the fundamental problem with the funds of funds as well as the hedge fund allocation industry as a whole. The investment committees do not have professionals who have traded capital and managed traders. Imagine that a football franchise wants to recruit new talent. Instead of sending the coaches to scout the talent, the franchise sends stadium builders, groundskeepers, and concession stand employees to do the scouting. As ludicrous as it sounds, that is what the fund of funds investment process is akin to.

I ran trading desks and managed several proprietary traders before I launched my own macro hedge fund. When I walked into my first meeting with a fund of funds, I expected to be grilled on the strategy and my knowledge of the markets by a group of senior traders who had traded in the macro space for several years. Instead, I met a group of individuals who sat down with stacks of papers with preprinted questions. Two hours later, after they had filled in the spaces in this questionnaire, I walked out with an allocation but felt that my investor had no clue about my strategy or my markets. The people I met with were more concerned with fitting me into one of their allocation buckets so they could satisfy their diversification criteria. I am sure that the only section of our monthly newsletter they cared to read was the section on returns. The sections describing our markets views and positions were duly filed under the "do not understand/care for" folder. It was quite amusing that after trading the CNY (Chinese Yuan) for more than a year and mentioning it in every monthly newsletter, a fund of funds asked me what CNY stood for.

The typical investor that decides to invest in a fund of funds is a pension fund, family office, or a University endowment. Many of these institutions have decided to not allocate internal resources but to outsource the hedge fund manager selection process to a fund of funds. These investors should want and demand that the outsourced party has the staff that understands the strategies they will be investing in. An understanding of the strategies that a fund of funds invests in will greatly reduce the chances of fraud as well. In the past weeks we have seen the largest Ponzi scheme in the financial industry unfold. I went to the website of one of the largest funds of funds that was invested in this scheme and took a look at the profiles of the investment professionals. To my dismay, I did not find one person on the Investment and Risk Management committee who has had any length of experience that would qualify him to understand and judge the trading strategies they were investing in.

A properly designed fund of funds can be a very useful allocation conduit in the hedge fund industry that can also justify the additional layer of fees it charges. A fund of funds investing panel should be comprised of senior trading managers from banks who have had firsthand experience trading the very strategies that they are investing in. In short, the model of a fund of funds should be the same as at a proprietary trading desk at a bank. At a typical proprietary trading desk, the head of the desk is a trader who has several years trading experience in the markets and managing traders. This head then has several traders reporting to him who trade their own strategies. On a daily basis the head of the desk sees and, more important, understands the risk of the entire group as well as the P/L statement. He further executes his own strategies, which can act to lever the strategies being deployed by his group of traders or hedge some of the exposure being taken by the traders. Furthermore, based on his understanding of the market conditions as well as the performance of the traders, he makes capital allocation decisions. This is a rational and information-driven allocation process rather than a process driven by backward-looking statistics, rumors, and herd mentality. A fund of funds designed like a proprietary trading group of a bank will have its own flavor and style, thereby providing returns that will be less correlated to the other fund of funds. This will also mean that a lot of the fund of funds will disappear because these funds never generated any real alpha via their investment process. A typical investor that invests in a fund of funds should demand real alpha, otherwise he or she is much better off investing in an investable hedge fund index or a multi-strategy hedge fund.

Some critics will say that some of the hedge funds do not offer the transparency, desired liquidity, or description of the strategy to implement the above-described model. First, the number of such funds was a select group to start with because most hedge funds do offer monthly liquidity and daily risk reporting. Additionally, after the recent market rout and a spate of frauds, a lot more hedge funds will be more than willing to increase transparency. At the end of the day, every legitimate hedge fund wants an educated and rational investor. If the hedge funds do not offer the requisite transparency or liquidity, I would suggest that the allocator move on to a hedge fund that does. If you did not know the color or make of a car, would you buy it? Then why would you invest billions in a strategy that you do not understand either? The recent financial crisis has proven that bigger and less transparent hedge funds do not fare any better than smaller and more transparent hedge funds. In fact, the larger institutions are more likely to put up gates and lock up capital when an investor wants his money back.

Monty Agarwal
Palm Beach Gardens, FL
magarwal@macmllc.com

CHAPTER 1

Recent Hedge Fund Scandals

PALM BEACH, FLORIDA

Palm Beach, Florida, is home to some of the highest net worth individuals in the country. This community has been investing in hedge funds for several decades and unfortunately has also been a target of several scam artists. As Palm Beach has featured in several financial scams and scandals in the press of late, it behooves me to delve a little bit deeper into the makeup of its denizens and the psychology of the society. I believe that it will help in understanding the way people generally approach investing and the overreliance on relationships rather than due diligence.

The island of Palm Beach is an exclusive community that runs about fourteen miles in length, but most of the multimillion-dollar mansions are located in a two-mile stretch along South Ocean Boulevard. It is often confused with West Palm Beach, but once you cross one of the three bridges connecting Palm Beach island to West Palm Beach you quickly realize that there is little in common between Palm Beach and what lies OTB ("over the bridge" in Palm Beach lingo). Palm Beach serves as a summer home for the super-rich Wall Street tycoons, industrialists, recording artists, and European aristocracy. While deserted almost six months of the summer, the height of the hurricane season in Florida, it comes to life from October to April. The lavish and umpteen charitable galas held every year at the Breakers Hotel and Donald Trump's Mar-a-Lago Club are a must-attend for the socialites of Palm Beach. My girlfriend at the time ran one of these charitable foundations on Palm Beach. As a result, we both frequented these charity balls. Being an outsider, I was often amused and befuddled by my observations. While sipping glasses of Dom Perignon and being entertained by crooners like Wayne Newton, the conversations often covered the latest exotic vacations, yacht acquisitions, and the best-performing investments of

the year. The competition to climb the social ladder in Palm Beach and being on the invitation "A" list is second to none. Being feted in the *Shiny
Sheet*, the Palm Beach society newspaper, by a charitable organization is far
more important than knowing the destination of one's philanthropic dollars. Need for social recognition and being a part of an exclusive group or
invitation list is a panacea. There is no wonder that in such an environment
a hedge fund that advertises superfluous or metronomic returns and admits
investors on an invitation-only basis would be highly sought after. As we
take a look at the following scandals, we will see that blind greed, a herd
mentality to belong to an exclusive club, and lack of proper due diligence
has often led to financial ruin.

KL FINANCIAL, MARCH 2005

John Kim, one of the founders of KL Financial, a hedge fund, once said, "I
cannot promise one hundred and fifty percent annual returns, but I won't
rule out the possibility." The story of KL Financial starts in a San Francisco
apartment in the late 1990s at the peak of the Internet boom and the day
trading fad. John Kim and Mr. Won Sok Lee, two of the three partners of
KL Financial, started day trading technology stocks. Neither of them had
any formal training or experience prior to this as stock traders. Mr. Lee
grew up in Las Vegas and earned a law degree at Tulane University in 1996.
He then worked as an associate in the gambling department at a Las Vegas
law firm, and, in the late 1990s, in the tax department at a San Diego law
firm. John Kim and his brother, the third partner, Yung Kim, grew up in a
Virginia suburb of Washington. John Kim often regaled his friends and
associates with the story of how upon graduating from George Washington
University he had operated a coffee importing business in South Korea, but
had it taken away by the despotic government because of its huge success.
No record of such a coffee importing business or its usurping by the South
Korean government can be found. Mr. Kim also liked to brag about his days
as a mergers and acquisition banker at Merrill Lynch, although Merrill
Lynch has no record of his ever working there. Furthermore, the NASD, a
regulator that licenses securities professionals, says it has no records that
any of the firm's three principals ever applied for the necessary licenses to
trade stocks for clients on Wall Street. Despite such a nebulous track record,
Mr. Kim and Mr. Lee rode the tech boom and managed to set up a trading
operation in Irvine, California, and in 2002 an office in Palm Beach, Florida. They hired a staff of inexperienced, usually fresh college graduates.
Mr. Kim acted as the Chief Investment Officer, his brother Yung Kim as the
Chief Financial Officer, and Mr. Lee handled back-office duties.

Ritzy Palm Beach Offices: Looking the Part

It is often said that if you want to be successful, you have to look the part. The principals of KL Financial took that to heart: When one is trying to woo the Palm Beach crowd, one has to really impress. They conjured up returns of 70 percent in 2003 and 40 percent in 2004, according to doctored statements given to investors. To complement their outsized returns, they bought outsized lifestyles. They bought flashy cars: Maserati, Porsche 911, and Mercedes SL 500. The firm's personal masseuse drove a Jaguar X-Type that was provided by KL Financial. End-of-year holiday parties were held in Las Vegas, where Mr. Kim and Mr. Lee were high-rolling VIPs at several casinos. They shopped on Worth Avenue, the equivalent of New York's Fifth Avenue and made themselves very conspicuous. They befriended the right people, who provided them with access to society functions and thereby introductions to their wealthy clients. To create the right impression, they spent $1.8 million in decorating their office space, which spanned most of the 17th floor of Esperante, a signature tower with bird's-eye views of KL Financial's target market: Palm Beach. According to a report by the *Palm Beach Post*, the $47,000-a-month suite's private landing had a $15,000 wall-size waterfall, a feng shui ceiling of carved wood and a floor of wenge planks, a dark, black-veined hardwood from Tanzania. The lobby had a rotunda-style coffered ceiling, dark mahogany built-ins, gray plush sofas, pewter-hued suede walls, and Wenge floors. Dakota Jackson custom furniture included Aldabhra conference room chairs of kiln-dried solid mahogany. Opposite a window wall overlooking the waterfront were double-faced wood-trimmed panels of frosted glass filled with reeds of bamboo. John Kim, the chief investment officer and senior principal had a $6,000 Inada black leather Shiatsu massage recliner in his spacious corner office. The large sunlit offices were filled with gorgeous desks designed by Dakota Jackson and a conference table that had to be hoisted seventeen floors through the building's elevator shaft. The trading floor had large flat-panel televisions scattered throughout. Spread on end tables and John Kim's credenza were brochures for Palm Beach, America's International Fine Art & Antique Fair, a book on Korean folk painting, and brochures for the Ritz-Carlton Golf Club, the Bear's Club, and PGA National Resort and Spa. John Kim's trading station had eighteen screens hooked up to ten computer towers. Former employees cooperating with the investigation told investigators that Kim's computers looked at times like rockets at liftoff, with lights blinking and fan motors revving. While KL Financial's offices were very expensively decorated, there are several hedge funds whose offices are even more stupendous. But the difference is that the principals of KL Financial used money stolen from its clients not earned in the markets.

Ronald Kochman: The Facilitator

Ronald Kochman has been mentioned in several press articles and investigator reports as the person instrumental in introducing the KL Financial principals to the Palm Beach elite. Since the late 1990s, Mr. Kochman had built a lucrative trusts-and-estates practice, counting a number of Palm Beach's movers and shakers as clients. "Kochman had one of the preeminent practices down here," said Richard Rampell, an accountant who worked with Mr. Kochman on several occasions. "In the last couple of years, he probated two estates that were well into nine or even ten figures. He was the envy of a lot of lawyers." According to investigators and KL employees, Mr. Kochman became increasingly involved with the firm and formed a close friendship with John Kim, who made Kochman a principal in KL Financial. Mr. Kochman, these people said, believed that there were greater riches to be reaped if KL were sold to a large Wall Street firm, as Mr. Kim indicated it eventually would be. They said Mr. Kochman planned to downsize his trusts-and-estates business in order to play an even bigger role at KL. Trusting his new friends, Mr. Kochman provided introductions to his clients and friends and was responsible for bringing in many of KL's investors, according to investigators. The aura of success and exclusivity around KL Financial was so strong that investors often begged to be let into its funds, some of which were said to have astounding annualized returns of 125 percent for several years. Among the funds' over two hundred investors were some of Palm Beach's elite, including Jerome Fisher, the founder of the Nine West shoe store chain; Carlos Morrison, an heir to the Fisher Body automotive fortune; and golf pros Nick Price and Raymond Floyd, according to people who have seen lists of investors.

The Duping and the Post Mortem

In the fall of 2004, several of KL Financial's investors started asking for certified audits of the funds. John Kim kept promising to get the audit done but kept delaying it. Investors started to get jittery and decided to redeem their assets. On February 22, 2005, Securities and Exchange Commission (SEC) officials unexpectedly visited KL Financial's offices and asked to see documents. After the meeting, investigators said, Mr. Lee walked out of the office, leaving a half-eaten bag of cookies on his desk. The next morning he went to the airport and bought a one-way ticket for South Korea, using frequent-flier miles. The day after that, Yung Kim disappeared as well. A few days after the SEC appeared on KL's doorstep, John Kim invited about thirty employees to his home. As the employees listened in shock, he said that the company was under investigation and that his brother and Mr. Lee were missing. John Kim squarely put the entire blame on his two partners and played the innocent victim.

KL Financial principals ran a Ponzi scheme, i.e., paying out any redemptions to existing investors from funds received from new investors. All the superfluous returns were doctored and $190 million of investors' money was either lost in the markets through incompetent trading activity or spent in personal pursuits by the principals.

On July 17, 2008, John Kim and his brother Yung Bae Kim were sentenced by the Honorable Kenneth L. Ryskamp in the United States District Court in West Palm Beach, Florida. John Kim was sentenced to 220 months imprisonment followed by three years of supervised release. Yung Bae Kim was sentenced to 75 months imprisonment followed by three years of supervised release. Each defendant was also ordered to pay restitution, which will consist of 50 percent of any income they earn in a Federal Prison Industries job, and following their release, ten percent of their monthly gross earnings. Won Lee, the third principal who is also named as a co-defendant in the indictment, remains a fugitive from justice.

The post mortem of the KL Financial in the presses produced the usual warnings from the various experts that went unheeded. First was the sloppy doctored re-creation of brokerage statements. The brokerage statements did not look professional and should have been spotted by the investors. Second, fingers were pointed at a lack of due diligence on John Kim's background. The offering memorandum of KL Financial did not give details on John Kim's professional background. And finally, the third red flag was the lack of audited statements.

These blatant red flags beg the question, How could such smart, successful and savvy investors from Palm Beach be duped by the charlatans of KL Financial? I feel that the answer to the question is twofold—an overreliance on relationships and not enough on due diligence; second and more important, improper due diligence. Many people have blamed greed for high returns as a culprit, which in my opinion is a ridiculous statement. We all have the option of keeping our money in cash or under the mattress.

My friend Steve Malone, a successful businessman, never invests in the stock market, let alone hedge funds. He invests in himself; he identifies businesses that he has a passion for, then he invests not just his money but time as well in these businesses. For those of us who do invest in the capital markets and hedge funds around the world, our main motivation for doing so is because we want higher returns while acknowledging that we are taking higher risks as well. The key is understanding all the risks involved in our investment decisions and then making prudent investment choices. The fault lies not with the desire to invest in high yielding investments but in not reconciling our expectations with the risks associated with them. The reason why the investors in KL Financial got duped was not because they were greedy but because they did not understand or care to find out all the risks involved in their investment.

Ronald Kochman was the estate and trust attorney for a lot of wealthy families on Palm Beach that invested in KL Financial. He was an attorney who was an expert in understanding the tax code, IRS regulations, and drawing up proper legal contracts to fulfill his clients' tax obligations. He was very good at that job, but how did that qualify him to become an expert on hedge fund trading strategies? What in Ronald Kochman's resume made his clients feel that he had the expertise to guide them toward a proper investment choice while explaining all the risks involved? Nothing. Ronald Kochman had excellent relationships with his clients built as a result of his work as an attorney for them. He used his relationships to open doors for KL Financial principals and to persuade his clients to invest with them. His clients put blind faith in their relationship with him and performed no due diligence. They should have hired experts who would have examined in great detail John Kim's trading models, their historical performance history, and the correlation of that performance with market cycles. Then they would have checked his trading background to verify his experience, education, and past performance, and finally they would have insisted on an audited track record. KL Financial would have never passed this rigorous due diligence process, and the investors would have been saved $190 million and Ronald Kochman his relationship with his clients.

AMARANTH ADVISORS, SEPTEMBER 2006

The everlasting red pigment of the Amaranth flower has stood as a symbol of immortality since the time of ancient Greece. Nicholas Maounis, the founder of Amaranth hedge fund picked the famed flower for the name of his hedge fund when he opened the fund in September 2000 with $600 hundred million in assets. Maounis graduated from the University of Connecticut in 1985 with a finance degree, started his career at investment bank LF Rothschild, Unterberg, Towbin and hedge fund Angelo, Gordon & Co., both based in New York. In 1992, he joined Greenwich-based Paloma Partners LLC, a hedge fund, and eventually traded $400 million, the largest amount managed by any individual at the hedge fund. After eight years, Maounis left to form Amaranth with twenty-seven employees. Based in Greenwich, Connecticut, Amaranth started out trading a convertible arbitrage strategy. Convertible bonds are bonds issued by companies that give the bond holder the option to buy the company's stock at a predetermined price. Convertible arbitrage traders profit from trading the perceived value of that embedded stock option. This strategy was Nick Maounis's expertise, what he knew best, and his original intention for starting his hedge fund.

Outgrowing Its Core Competency

Amaranth flourished, and the fund was able to attract big money from some of the biggest institutional investors, including funds run by Goldman Sachs Group Inc., Morgan Stanley, Deutsche Bank AG, and Bank of New York Co.'s Ivy Asset Management Corp. Pension funds of 3M Co. of St. Paul, Minnesota, and the San Diego County public employees also signed on. At its peak, according to Amaranth's marketing materials, it described itself as a global, multi-strategy hedge fund. Amaranth had over 400 employees, including 170 investment professionals, and managed in excess of $9 billion for institutional investors, including corporate and public pension funds, endowments and foundations, insurance companies, banks, family offices, and funds of hedge funds. The basic rule of capitalism is that money will flow where there are the biggest money-making opportunities or inefficiencies. Money will keep flowing until those inefficiencies have been taken out of the market. This is what happened to the convertible arbitrage market in the early 2000s and why Nick Maounis decided to diversify his ever-growing hedge fund into other areas.

Brian Hunter

The area that Nick Maounis picked was energy trading, and the trader he picked to run that area was Brian Hunter, a 26-year-old trader. Hunter, who grew up near Calgary, had earned a master's degree in mathematics from the University of Alberta before starting to trade natural gas in 1998, according to Amaranth marketing materials. He traded for Calgary-based TransCanada Corp., then joined Deutsche Bank in New York in May 2001. In his first two years, he earned $69 million for the bank, according to a complaint Hunter later filed in New York State court in Manhattan that claims the bank owes him bonus money. By 2003, Hunter was head of the bank's natural gas desk. In December 2003, Hunter and his colleagues were up $76 million for the year. In the first week of the month, however, the desk lost $51 million after an "unprecedented and unforeseeable run-up in gas prices," according to Hunter's lawsuit. Hunter says in the suit that even with the loss, he made $40 million for Deutsche Bank that year and more than $100 million in three years. Hunter left Deutsche Bank in April 2004 and joined Amaranth shortly thereafter. According to former employees, by the end of 2005, Hunter was the highest paid trader at Amaranth. Hunter earned 15 percent of any profit he made, while most traders made an average of 10 percent. In 2005, Hunter took home about $75 million, primarily from his Katrina bet, compared with about $4 million in 2004. At the end of 2005, Maounis let Hunter move his wife and two children back to Calgary and open an office with eight traders. By this time, Brian Hunter was running by far the largest risk position in Amaranth's $9 billion fund and was concentrated in the natural gas market. So much for the diversified, global multi-strategy fund, as Amaranth advertised itself.

Risk Management Failure

In the month of September 2006, Amaranth lost $6 billion or 65 percent of the fund's capital on a single natural gas trade. Hunter speculated on the direction of natural gas price based on weather and hurricane forecasting and placed most of his trades in the futures market over NYMEX. Futures contracts are derivative instruments that let you leverage your bet. Given the way the initial margins were structured, you could hold a position with a $100 exposure with only $12.50 in actual capital, thereby giving you an eight to one leverage. In 2005 Hunter made a lot of money when hurricanes Katrina and Rita caused massive spikes in natural gas prices. In September 2006, Hunter bet on a repeat of 2005 hurricane season and took long positions in natural gas futures contracts. The exact composition of his trades is not known. By the third week of 2006, as the sun shone brightly on the Gulf of Mexico and there was no sign of any impending storms, the price of natural gas started to fall precipitously. During the second week of September 2006, the natural gas contract broke through an important price support level at $5.50 and proceeded to drop another 20 percent in a two-week period. As the price of natural gas continued to drop, Amaranth's losses grew to $6 billion.

Amaranth was not a fly-by-night Ponzi scheme like KL Financial that I discussed earlier. It started out as a $600 million convertible arbitrage strategy run by a trader who was an expert in his field. It had a reputable auditor, and the fund would have passed on all due diligence metrics. After all, it did receive capital from some of the most well-respected institutional investors who are known for conducting rigorous due diligence, like banks and pension funds. So what went wrong and when did it start going wrong? It was not until 2004 when Amaranth had grown substantially bigger than $600 million, and the opportunities in convertible arbitrage had dried up, that Amaranth started to lose its way. Nick Maounis wanted to model his hedge fund on Ken Griffin's multi-strategy $20 billion fund, Citadel. Citadel runs at least twenty independent strategies across its funds managed by different portfolio managers. The risk and capital are well distributed across these strategies. Amaranth chased Brian Hunter's short-term track record and became invested almost 100 percent in the long natural gas trade. At least one diligent investor did spot this. "It looked to us like the Amaranth multi-strategy fund was a pure energy bet," says Edward Vasser, chief investment officer of Wolf Asset Management International LLC, a Santa Fe, New Mexico-based fund of funds. "Almost all of their profits came from their energy portfolio." He decided against investing in Amaranth, but several other investors blindly followed Amaranth's track record and jumped in with an additional $379 million in June 2006, the biggest inflow of the year, according to an Amaranth document given to investors. The firm's energy allocation was unchanged as of July 31, according to an investor letter sent in August. "While we are targeting a smaller allocation for natural gas in the future, we believe opportunities in the natural gas market remain attractive and continue to maintain positions where we believe fundamentals are disconnected with current prices." A month later Amaranth had lost 65 percent of its capital and all on one trade.

Here in lies a very important lesson in hedge fund investing. As any other traditional investment needs to be monitored on a regular basis, so do hedge fund investments. Most investors, even the most diligent ones, tend to perform their due diligence at the onset of the investment and then as long as the returns are good, they do not care to keep track of capital growth, strategy shifts, or risk management. In fact, given the esoteric nature of the strategies deployed at hedge funds, the level of ongoing due diligence has to be meticulously performed by qualified people. As Amaranth grew in capital and the opportunities in the convertible arbitrage market shrank, Amaranth changed its strategy. It produced 15 percent returns when other multi-strategy hedge funds were producing 5 percent returns over the same period of time. This should have been a red flag; instead, it caused investors to throw more money at Amaranth. As Ed Vasser of Wolf Asset Management discovered, most investors would have realized that Amaranth was far from a well-diversified multi-strategy fund. It was betting the pensions of 3M Co. and the San Diego County public employees on one trader and one trade. It might have had better odds at a craps table in Vegas, and the drinks would have been free as well.

BERNIE MADOFF, DECEMBER 2008

As I write this book, the Bernie Madoff Ponzi scheme is unfolding before our eyes. When KL Financial lost $190 million in its Ponzi scheme back in 2005, it was billed as the largest financial scam in history. Bernie Madoff's $65 billion Ponzi scheme over the course of the last 15 years easily tops that.

Senio Figliozzi, owner of the Everglades Barber Shop in Palm Beach, cut Bernie Madoff's hair, gave him facials, manicures, and pedicures for seventeen years and described him as a "very nice man who was always polite and gentlemanly" and tipped the standard 20 percent. Bernie Madoff was described as low key. The Madoffs rarely appeared at major Palm Beach charity balls, the island's chief vehicle for social climbing. Some of Mr. Madoff's sales agents, who recruited investors, also had little contact with him. As Charles Gradante, a hedge fund adviser who met him regularly on the Palm Beach social circuit, observed, "When I saw him at cocktail parties, he would be in the corner and investors would sometimes go over to him. He didn't have a charismatic presence; he wasn't exuding confidence."

Bernie Madoff worked as a lifeguard on Rockaway Beach, on the edge of New York, and installed sprinkler systems. After receiving his undergraduate degree from Hofstra University in 1960, at the age of 21, he founded Bernard L. Madoff Securities LLC with the $5,000 he had managed to save up working as a lifeguard and doing other odd jobs. Mr. Madoff's firm, like several at the time, was known as a "third market" trading company—buying and selling stocks that weren't listed on the NYSE. Mr. Madoff got his big break in 1975, when fixed commissions for stock trades were abolished. This allowed him to trade blue-chip stocks on the Big Board that had once been off limits to non-member firms such as his. Mr. Madoff handled large blocks of trades for brokerage giants A.G. Edwards & Sons and Charles Schwab & Co and profited from small commissions per share.

By the 1990s, Bernie Madoff had built a successful and reputable stock trading operation. On certain days his firm was handling close to 10 percent of NASDAQ shares. His firm's competitive advantage came from the technology platform he built with help from his younger brother Peter. Cerebral and reserved, Peter Madoff joined the company in 1970 after graduating from law school. With the system, traders at other firms could electronically buy and sell at the best prices available on NASDAQ. The Madoff brothers seemed to make a good team, with Bernie the trader and Peter the technician. By the late 1980s, the firm moved from Wall Street to the gleaming Lipstick Building on Third Avenue, a granite and steel clad tower designed by famed architect Philip Johnson. At first, the company occupied two of the building's 34 floors, with the trading operations on the eighteenth floor and his money-management operation one floor below. Mr. Madoff's two sons joined the firm after graduation as well, starting out as entry-level trading.

Bernie the Broker Overnight Becomes a Derivatives Trader

Bernie Madoff spent a lot of time in Washington lobbying for moving more of the trading from the stock exchange floor to an electronic platform. He also became more involved in NASDAQ and was appointed its nonexecutive chairman in 1990, 1991, and 1993. He used this success and the cachet of being appointed the chairman of the NASDAQ to launch his asset management business in the 1990s. Bernie had no trading strategy, technical trading models, or intention of investing his client's capital. He had been an executing broker his entire career and had made his money through commissions. Given his successful career thus far and the reputation he had earned, one has to assume that Bernie started out with good intentions of investing his client's capital and then somehow something went horribly wrong that sent him down the path of ruin. No rational person would ever imagine that he or she could get away with a Ponzi scheme, and he had worked too hard to simply want to throw it all away. Details of the scandal are still emerging, and I am sure we will learn more about what actually happened behind the scenes over the years to come.

Bernie started out with friends' and family's capital, like most startup hedge funds do. He advertised 10 to 12 percent steady returns for years and naturally started to attract attention from the investors. When I started my hedge fund in 2004, an industry advisor and friend told me that all I had to do was produce 1 percent net returns a month and I would raise more capital than I could handle. After all, if somebody told you that you could earn 12 percent returns a year with little or no risk, why would you invest your money in government bonds that yield 3 percent right now or the stock market, which has produced only a 6.5 percent annualized return with massive volatility? Heck, you would even want to borrow money at 5 percent and invest in a strategy that delivered you 12 percent year after year—it would only be good economics.

The investing community bought into Bernie's story hook, line, and sinker. High net worth individuals, pension funds, banks, and endowments started lining up to invest in Bernie Madoff. He had a stellar reputation in the markets and was promising and delivering metronomic returns. Bernie also understood the human psyche extremely well. He knew that perception was reality, and the more you shrouded that perception in a cloak of mystery and opaqueness, the more vehemently people would believe in it. To perpetuate this mystique, he refused to answer, in any detail, questions regarding his strategy. Bernie not just avoided his investors but also his own marketers who were responsible for raising capital for his fund. Over a 15-year period, Mr. Spring, one of his agents in Boca Raton, Florida, had only eight or ten brief meetings with Mr. Madoff, according to one person familiar with their relationship. Eli Budd, a former Minnesota accountant who worked with some of Mr. Madoff's investors, said he only met Mr. Madoff once or twice. Mr. Madoff also could be inaccessible to bankers who were interested in helping potential investors. "You couldn't meet Madoff. He was like a pop star," said one banker who was considering offering loans to customers so they could invest in Mr. Madoff's funds.

Palm Beach Connection and Robert Jaffe

On Wall Street, any money-making strategy attracts not just a lot of capital but also middlemen. Bernie Madoff signified the latest gold rush, and men like Robert Jaffe of Palm Beach jumped in to sell shovels. Robert Jaffe and his wife Ellen were big names in Palm Beach social circles. Robert Jaffe was on the boards of the Palm Healthcare Foundation, the Palm Beach Chapter of the American Cancer Society, the Palm Beach Civic Association, and the Morse Life foundation. His wife Ellen sat on the board of the Kravis Center, the local performing arts center, and both of them were major fundraisers for the Dana-Farber Cancer Institute of Boston. Robert Jaffe shared a business relationship with Bernie Madoff through New York based Cohmad Securities Corp. Robert Jaffe was a vice president and principal of Cohmad, and "mad" in Cohmad stood for Madoff. The Massachusetts secretary of state subpoenaed company records in January 2009 to try to figure out its relationship with Madoff Investment Securities. In June 2009, the SEC finally charged Robert Jaffe and two other principals of Cohmad Securities Corp. with fraud. According to the court documents, Cohmad Securities Corp. acted as a marketing firm for Madoff and in the process collected more than $10 million in fees since 2000. This was in addition to the fees paid directly to Robert Jaffe, which were in excess of $10 million. Robert and Bernie not only shared a business relationship, but they also lived within a thousand feet of each other—Madoff in a $10 million home and Jaffe in a $17 million mansion on North Lake Way on Palm Beach Island. They also belonged to the same country club, the Palm Beach Country Club, with annual membership dues of $350,000.

People on Palm Beach were so drunk on the Madoff Kool-Aid that they joined the Palm Beach Country club, paying the massive annual membership dues, so they could be introduced to Bernie Madoff, often through Robert Jaffe. "He was the man you went to, to get to Madoff. You had to grovel," said one club member, who, like most, declined to let his name be used for fear of being ostracized at the club. Richard Rampell, a CPA whose clients include those who lost millions in the scheme, said it was common knowledge that Jaffe was the go-to guy for those who wanted to invest with Madoff. Robert Jaffe does not deny this relationship either. In an interview with *The Palm Beach Daily News*, Jaffe readily admitted that he would introduce potential clients to Bernie Madoff and earn a fee for consummating the transaction. Jaffe described his take as "common practice in the business." At a party in February 2009 at Mar-a-Lago, just a few weeks after the Madoff scheme became public, Nine West shoes founder Jerome Fisher lashed into Jaffe. "You've got a lot of nerve showing up here!" Fisher told Jaffe, according to others at the party. By the way, this is the same Jerome Fisher who was also invested in KL Financial. Within a week of the Madoff scandal, four multimillion-dollar condominiums at Two Breakers Row, a complex just north of the landmark Breakers hotel, were put up for sale by owners who invested with Mr. Madoff, said Nadine House, a real-estate agent here. In a telephone interview recently, one of the Madoff investors said, "We went to sleep rich with a $140 million in the bank and woke up completely broke." I guess money invested with Madoff was not necessarily money in the bank, but prior to December 11, 2008 that was the perception. This investor recently put his house on the market as well.

Conclusion: Failure of the So-Called Experts: The Funds of Funds

Madoff's mystique, steady returns, and the never-ending quest of wealthy Palm Beach investors to belong to the latest exclusive club ensured that Madoff had his steady supply of new capital from the high net worth community. But what is absolutely mind-boggling is the fact that so-called experts in the field of hedge fund investing, the funds of hedge funds, also were completely duped by Madoff's Ponzi scheme. Funds of hedge funds are supposed to be experts at conducting due diligence on hedge fund managers and understanding their strategies. Some of the biggest funds of hedge funds in the industry, like Mass Mutual, owned Tremont Capital Management, Ezra Merkin's Ascot Partners, and Fairfield Greenwich Group completely failed in their fiduciary responsibilities to their investors in conducting appropriate due diligence on Madoff. The list of high-profile investors that invested in Madoff is endless. Even the famous Hollywood director Steven Spielberg's Wunderkinder foundation was completely let down by the so-called expert advisors who decided to invest its money with Madoff.

J. Ezra Merkin, the former chairman of lender GMAC, also is head of Gabriel Partners, a $5 billion money-management firm whose clients include wealthy families and university endowments. One of Mr. Merkin's funds, the $1.8 billion Ascot Partners LP, had substantially all of its assets invested with Mr. Madoff, according to a letter from Mr. Merkin sent to clients. Several Ascot clients say they had no idea that Mr. Merkin had most of the fund's money invested with Mr. Madoff. One Ascot investor was a charitable trust established by real-estate magnate Mortimer Zuckerman, the chairman of real-estate firm Boston Properties and owner of the

New York Daily News and *U.S. News & World Report*. In a recent interview on the Fox News Channel, Mr. Zuckerman said he had no idea that such a large amount of money was invested with Mr. Madoff through one fund. Ascot Partners basically channeled its client's capital to Madoff and charged a whopping 1.5 percent annual management fee for that privilege. It conducted no meaningful due diligence on his strategy, which is the primary responsibility of a fund of hedge funds. By investing the entire sum with one manager, it did not diversify the risk on its clients' capital, another responsibility of a fund of funds. It also conducted no meaningful due diligence on its operations, otherwise it would have realized that Madoff's accountant was a small three-person shop with prior links to Madoff.

Fairfield Greenwich, a $14 billion fund of hedge funds, had half of its assets or $7.5 billion, invested with Madoff. This lucrative relationship earned Fairfield Greenwich $160 million in 2007 alone and ended up costing its investors $7.5 billion. Walter Noel, the founder of Fairfield Greenwich group, was a master at raising capital from its vast network of global contacts. His four sons-in-law had connections among the wealthy in Rio de Janeiro, Madrid, Milan, London, and Geneva, who brought socialite flair and few demanding questions for Mr. Madoff. I decided to pay a visit to the Fairfield Greenwich group website, www.fggus.com, for a peek at its due diligence process. The following two out of over twenty bullet points in Fairfield Greenwich's due diligence process would have been sufficient to assess that Madoff's strategy was infeasible and his returns doctored:

- Conducts detailed interviews to better understand the manager's methodology for forming a market view, and for selecting and exiting core positions
- Performance return in calm versus volatile markets

But quite clearly, stating a due diligence process and actually conducting it are two completely different processes. Fairfield Greenwich Group did not fulfill its fiduciary responsibilities by conducting its own stated due diligence process, otherwise Madoff's strategy and track record would not have stood up to the scrutiny.

Split Strike Convergence

Madoff's strategy was simply termed as "split-strike convergence," which in simple terms meant buying the S&P 100 index and giving up some of the upside for downside protection. Let us assume that at the start of a given month, the S&P 100 index was at 900. Madoff's strategy involved buying the index at 900, buying downside protection say 2 percent lower, index

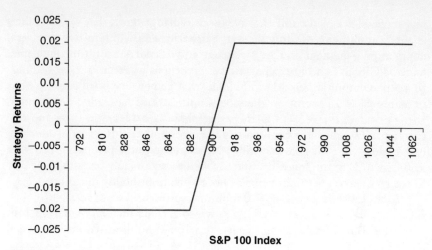

FIGURE 1.1 Madoff's strategy return chart.

value of 882, and selling the upside 2 percent higher, index value of 918. Let us further assume that the volatility structure allowed the purchase of the put and the selling of the call option to be at a net zero cost. Assuming no leverage in the portfolio, his return chart would look like Figure 1.1. The strategy would make no more than 2 percent in any given month that the market went up, and the strategy would lose no more than 2 percent in any given month the market went down either. This implies that Madoff's strategy would have only performed in the periods that the stock market went up. A study of the S&P 100 monthly data over the last 10 years, 1999 to 2008, shows that the S&P 100 was up 63 months and down 57 months. Any level of in-depth due diligence would have shown that Madoff's strategy could not have produced the steady unerring returns of 10 to 12 percent over that period by executing his split-strike convergence strategy. Therefore, most likely what happened was that strategy due diligence was never conducted and Madoff's reputation and stature was deemed sufficient.

The Mystery of the Missing $65 Billion

As the investigators pour over all the data and try to piece the missing clues together, the big question in everybody's mind is what happened to the missing $65 billion. Madoff hardly ever traded the capital; therefore, it is unlikely that the money was actually lost in the markets. Over the course of 19 years, from the early 1990s onwards, Madoff reported 10 to 12 percent net returns. While most investors left their capital with Madoff and let it compound, very few investors took out the returns and the capital investments. We also know that the funds of hedge funds that invested their clients' capital with Madoff charged hefty fees. Fairfield Greenwich capital charged management fees of 1 percent and 20 percent of annual profits. Kingate Global Fund Ltd., charged 1.5 percent of assets a year, in addition to a 5 percent initial fee. Madoff claims that he got paid with commissions of as much as 3 percent on the stocks and options he traded per annum. Using this data I have put together, the following tables show how most of the capital would have been paid out in fees to Madoff and the funds of hedge funds over the course of time. Now it is up to the prosecutors to look at the records of the funds of funds as well to try to claw back the fees collected by them on fictitious returns, not to mention shoddy due diligence.

Table 1.1 shows how a $100 million investment with Madoff through a fund of funds would have trickled down to zero by the end of year eleven. Over the course of the eleven years, nearly $49 million would have been

TABLE 1.1   Fees and Commissions Collected on $100 mm by Madoff and Feeder Funds

Net Reported Returns	11.00%
Madoff Annual Commissions	3.00%
Feeder Management Fees	1.00%
Feeder Performance Fees	15.00%

Year	Reported Capital	Fees Collected by Madoff	Fees Collected by Funds of Funds	Real Capital
0	$100.00			$100.00
1	$107.42	$3.00	$3.02	$ 93.98
2	$115.40	$3.22	$3.24	$ 87.52
3	$123.97	$3.46	$3.48	$ 80.58
4	$133.17	$3.72	$3.74	$ 73.12
5	$143.06	$4.00	$4.02	$ 65.11
6	$153.68	$4.29	$4.31	$ 56.50
7	$165.09	$4.61	$4.63	$ 47.26
8	$177.34	$4.95	$4.98	$ 37.33
9	$190.51	$5.32	$5.35	$ 26.66
10	$204.65	$5.72	$5.75	$ 15.20
11	$219.84	$6.14	$6.17	$ 2.89
		$48.43	$48.69	

collected by Madoff in fees, and another $49 million by the funds of funds. The calculations assume that no capital or returns are redeemed by investors, and there were no losses or gains from any investment activity.

Table 1.2 shows how a $100 million investment made directly with Madoff without involving a middleman would have trickled down to zero by the end of year 15. Over the course of the 15 years, nearly $100 million would have been collected by Madoff in fees. The calculations assume that no capital or returns are redeemed by investors, and there were no losses or gains from any investment activity.

There are several takeaways from looking at the calculations in the above displayed tables. The first is that the sum of $65 billion was a fictional amount that was reported based on doctored net returns of 10 to 12 percent a year. The reality is that the total amount of capital invested with Bernie

TABLE 1.2 Commissions Collected on $100 mm by Madoff

Net Reported Returns			11.00%
Madoff Annual Commissions			3.00%

Yr	Reported Capital	Fees Collected by Madoff	Real Capital
0	$100.00		$100.00
1	$110.58	$3.00	$ 97.00
2	$122.28	$3.32	$ 93.68
3	$135.22	$3.67	$ 90.01
4	$149.52	$4.06	$ 85.96
5	$165.34	$4.49	$ 81.47
6	$182.84	$4.96	$ 76.51
7	$202.18	$5.49	$ 71.03
8	$223.57	$6.07	$ 64.96
9	$247.22	$6.71	$ 58.25
10	$273.38	$7.42	$ 50.84
11	$302.30	$8.20	$ 42.64
12	$334.29	$9.07	$ 33.57
13	$369.65	$10.03	$ 23.54
14	$408.76	$11.09	$ 12.45
15	$452.01	$12.26	$ 0.19
		$99.81	

Madoff never grew but kept dwindling down toward zero as it was paid out in fees and commissions. It is very likely that some of the invested capital was paid out to investors as principal or return redemptions as well, but, as the calculations above show, most of that money is still either with Bernie Madoff or has been paid in fees to the middlemen like the fund of funds.

LESSON 1: RELATIONSHIPS DO NOT TRUMP DUE DILIGENCE

The three recent hedge fund implosions and outright scandals described above are a small subset of the poor investment decisions made by investors over the course of time. The lessons from these mistakes are few but occur with very high frequency. In too many cases, individual high net worth investors have relied on personal relationships and not on due diligence in making an investment. Investing your hard-earned money is not a hobby and should not be treated as one, especially when investing in an esoteric strategy that is not transparent. Too often we have seen cases where well-educated and successful businessmen have relied on their golfing and country club buddies to become their investment guides. Just because your golfing buddy of twenty years or a well-respected socialite is investing in a particular strategy does not mean that you should blindly follow them as well. You might end up losing not just your hard-earned money but also your golfing buddy of twenty years. Often we see such people conducting more due diligence on buying a $100,000 car than putting $10 million in an investment strategy.

LESSON 2: WHEN INVESTING IN HEDGE FUNDS, HIRE EXPERTS

The second lesson for high net worth individuals that can to be drawn is that there is a big difference between investing and trading. Buying stocks or investing in a long-only mutual fund is not the same as investing in a hedge fund. You would not ask your local pharmacist to perform a surgery or buy a do-it-yourself kit, you would research and find an expert surgeon. Hedge fund strategies are complex, risks myriad and ever evolving. Hedge funds are constantly trading the capital; they might change the portfolio direction several times a month, deploy leverage, sell volatility to collect premium, and take other risks that would not be obvious in any offering memorandum or in any monthly newsletter. Such risks can only be determined by experts who have traded similar strategies and are familiar with the risks to ask the right questions. I wish I could tell the reader that his or her hedge fund investment would be safe if he or she just avoided managers with short track records, superfluous and steady returns, or no-name auditors. Hedge fund investments are a lot more involved than that and thereby require a great deal of initial as well as ongoing due diligence. There is much discussion on proper due diligence of a hedge fund manager as well as on going monitoring of hedge funds in later chapters. Therefore, I would highly recommend that any high net worth individual investor who is considering investing in a hedge fund seek out appropriate advisors and consultants. My consulting firm, MACM Hedge Fund Consulting, www.MACMLLC.com does offer these services to the retail as well as the institutional investor.

LESSON 3: "WE DID NOT KNOW WHAT WE WERE INVESTING IN" IS NOT AN EXCUSE

It seems like with every scandal or big market loss we hear the common excuse from investors, "We did not know what we were investing in, therefore the blame must be put on somebody else." When the credit markets were awash with cash, homebuyers took out ARMs so they could buy a $1 million house while making a $50,000 salary. Investors bought credit-related securities that provided a 10 percent yield because they did not want to buy government securities that provided a 5 percent yield. Investors bought into Madoff's steady 12 percent returns a year because they did not want to stomach the gyrations of the stock market. All these decisions were made consciously and willingly by the investors and not forced upon them by any government entity. Maybe they were marketed aggressively, but that is a basic precept of a market-based economy. The investor always has the option to take the safer route and invest his or her money in a government bond or buy a house with a 30-year fixed mortgage. The reason we invest in stocks and alternative investments or buy a house with an adjustable rate mortgage is because we want higher returns or a better life style while acknowledging that we are taking higher risks as well. The key is to understand all the risks involved in our investment decisions and then make prudent investment choices. If later it turns out that our choices were not prudent, we only have ourselves to blame for them.

CONCLUSION: SO CALLED EXPERTS, FUND OF FUNDS, HAVE FAILED

Another startling observation, especially from the Madoff scandal has been the ineptitude of some of these so-called experts on hedge fund strategies, the funds of funds. Several high net worth individuals, university endowments, and charitable foundations did the right thing by employing funds of funds to conduct due diligence on their behalf. But, as we can see from the failure of Fairfield Greenwich Group, Tremont Holdings, Ascot Partners, and others that the funds of funds did not conduct appropriate due diligence on Madoff either. Walter Noel of Fairfield Greenwich was very capable at raising capital for his fund of funds. He came from a management consulting and private banking background. His expertise was establishing and maintaining relationships with the wealthy investors around the world. His founding partner, Jeff Tucker was a lawyer by training. In fact, taking a look at the senior members of Fairfield Greenwich team, I could not find one person who had the requisite trading background to be able to properly assess the trading strategies that the company was investing in. Fairfield Greenwich confused its asset-raising ability for its asset-investing ability. This common problem can be seen throughout the funds of funds industry, where the institutions are very capable of raising capital but do not possess the proper expertise to deploy it effectively. We will explore this broken model and discuss how to fix it in later chapters.

CHAPTER 2

The Players

If you wanted to invest in the stock market or an ETF (exchange traded fund), you could simply log into your E-Trade or Schwab account and within seconds fire off a trade and become an investor in Dell. The entire process would cost you no more than a few cents per stock, and you would not need to read and sign reams of papers acknowledging that you knew and understood all the risks you were taking. Furthermore, like any diligent investor, you could follows all the news on Dell in newspapers, business news channels, conference calls, analyst reports, or any of the other sources and feel that you knew exactly where your hard-earned money was invested and how it was likely to perform. But, most important, say if you woke up one day and realized that Dell was going to have a hard time competing with the latest brainchild of Steve Jobs, you could very easily pay a few more cents and within seconds sell your Dell and become a proud owner of Apple stock. Analyzing, buying, and selling stocks or even bonds and money market funds is a transparent, cheap, and easy process; investing in hedge funds is a lot more complex than that.

Total hedge fund industry assets reached $2 trillion as of December 31, 2007. There are approximately 9,400 hedge funds and 1,600 funds of hedge funds in the world today. Net asset flows into hedge funds are increasing dramatically, largely due to institutional allocations. Investing in hedge funds is not a transparent, cheap, or easy process by any means. The hedge fund industry has been described as highly secretive, expensive, risky, and hard to access. There are layers of middlemen in the form of consultants, advisors, fund of funds, and third-party marketers who have made fortunes trying to match investors with the appropriate hedge fund managers. The middlemen's main responsibility has been to understand the hedge fund strategies and make the hedge funds less opaque to the end investors. In my opinion, most of the middlemen have completely failed at this task. In the later chapters we will explore how the so-called experts have failed at their jobs and what needs to be done to fix it. For any hedge fund investor, it is very important to understand the layout of the hedge fund industry and the various layers involved. To get a better idea of these different layers, I have presented the following flowchart of investment dollars in the hedge fund industry and the various layers of middlemen involved in the process.

FLOW OF CAPITAL IN THE HEDGE FUND INDUSTRY

The first layer comprises the end investor. The pension funds, high net worth Individuals (HNWs), banks, and endowments are the people with the money who have made the decision to invest in hedge funds. Sometimes these investors will invest directly in the hedge funds, but most of the time they will outsource the due diligence and hedge fund picking activity to an expert, like a fund of funds. A fund of hedge funds, as the name suggests, invests not in any underlying security but in a portfolio of hedge funds in order to provide diversification and thereby provide lower volatility returns than a single hedge fund would. A typical fund of funds will invest in ten to sometimes over a hundred individual hedge funds. The investors feel they do not have the requisite expertise to decide on the right hedge fund investments and how to evaluate the entry and exit points; therefore, they rely on the funds of funds to provide that expertise (see Figure 2.1).

Pension Funds

The pension funds are perhaps the most influential group of investors in hedge funds. Receiving a capital investment from a pension fund is considered a vote of approval by a hedge fund or a fund of funds. Pension funds have traditionally set very high bars for hedge fund managers in terms of stability of returns, infrastructure, and general due diligence. Pension funds are also highly sought after by the hedge fund managers because they are considered stable investors who tend to stay with the hedge funds through up and down cycles.

This group of investors comprises the pension funds of publicly traded companies as well as government entities. Pension fund investing in hedge funds is a global phenomenon. Except for the Slovak Republic and Mexico, all other countries allow pension fund investing in hedge funds. Although the level of investment is still very low in other countries, it is almost universally expected to increase. Although estimates vary, up to 20 percent of European and American pension funds and 40 percent of Japanese pension funds are believed to invest in hedge funds.

Most states in the United States have pension liabilities for teachers, firefighters, utility workers, and other government employees. Approximately

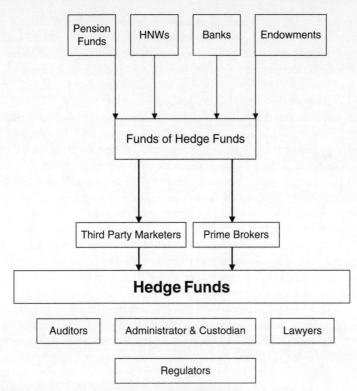

FIGURE 2.1   Flow of capital in the hedge fund industry.

2,300 public employee pension plans with more than $2 trillion in assets cover some 15 million state and local government workers nationwide. State pension funds invest their capital in stocks, bonds, cash, private equity, real estate, and hedge funds. These funds have pension liabilities that are rarely 100 percent funded, and they rely on investment returns to bridge that gap. A 2006 survey of 125 state retirement systems by Wilshire Research shows the breadth and magnitude of the problem. Of the 58 plans that provided actuarial data for 2005, 84 percent of them were underfunded. For those providing data for 2004, the number was even higher at 87 percent. This is up from 79 percent in 2002 and 51 percent in 2001. Under current investment strategies and a standard equity premium of 6.5 percent, there is a two-thirds chance that states pension plans will realize a shortfall in 15 years. The expected conditional shortfall is almost $1.5 trillion. This research is a major reason why pension funds have to reach for returns larger than 6.5 percent, and the best place they feel they can find this kind of return is in the alternative investment space of hedge funds. Perhaps the two largest government pension funds that invest in hedge funds are California Public Employees' Retirement System (CalPERS) with a total market value as of January 2, 2009 of $188 billion and Ontario Teachers Pension Plan (OTPP) with $108 billion in net assets.

Corporate defined pension plans have also been hit hard by the sharp declines in the global stock markets in 2008. Standard & Poor's estimated corporate retirement coffers in aggregate may end the year 2008 with a shortfall of more than $219 billion. The pension problem is particularly acute in the energy sector because the group is comprised of older companies who are still required to make contributions to a defined plan while newer companies have switched to undefined benefit plans like 401(k)s.

Traditional investments in the equity markets are exposed to severe market downturns and bear markets. Hedge funds can be used to manage, reduce, and indeed hedge such risks. Because hedge funds have the flexibility of going long, short, and even leveraging their bets or concentrating on a particular sector of the market, they are perceived to have the ability to provide positive returns in a bull or bear market. In addition, pension funds are progressively more prepared to invest in a broader range of global products—from emerging market debt or equity, high yield fixed income, currencies, property, commodities, illiquid investments, and so on. Hedge funds are increasingly used as instruments to facilitate this new investment approach. As mentioned earlier, some pension funds are invested in hedge funds directly as a result of their own research, understanding, and due diligence, while most rely exclusively on funds of funds to provide this critical service. A pension fund that was invested directly with Bernie Madoff's hedge fund was the Town of Fairfield, Connecticut, Employees Pension Fund. The Connecticut pension fund said it had about $40 million managed by Madoff. It is unknown whether the Connecticut pension fund had the requisite expertise to conduct thorough due diligence on Madoff's strategy or whether it got taken in by Madoff's reputation and steady doctored returns.

High Net Worth Individuals (HNWs)

The definition of a high net worth individual is highly fluid and changes with geography, nationality, and passage of time. Every country has its own regulations, but for the United States an individual who is qualified to invest in a hedge fund must meet one of the following two criteria. Because hedge funds do not fall under the purview of the SEC, the government has deemed hedge funds as only suitable for sophisticated investors. These investors do not need the protection that comes with the regulations on mutual funds. These wealthy individuals must pass either an accredited investor test or a qualified purchaser test. An *accredited investor* is an individual who either has a net worth greater than $1 million and has an income in the past two years that exceeds $200,000 a year and expects to continue this way or holds assets greater than $5 million. A *qualified purchaser* is either an individual who owns at least $5 million in investments or a family-held business that owns at least $5 million in investments or a business that has discretion of at least $25 million in investments or a trust that is sponsored by qualified purchasers.

The ultra-rich individual investors who have assets higher than $50 million tend to create *family offices*. These family offices serve the dual function of managing the wealth from a return as well as tax perspective. These family offices then decide to invest in traditional equity and bond markets as well as in the alternative investment space of hedge funds. The basic goal of every family office is to pool the resources of an extended family under one umbrella to achieve higher levels of wealth management. The family office uses in-house as well as outsourced resources to meet the financial goals as well as tax obligations of the family. Often, this customized support allows for the pursuit of a family's non-financial agenda as well, including strategic philanthropy.

Even after a year like 2008 when the average hedge fund was down over 20 percent, the family offices are still showing their faith in hedge funds. Over the past five years, family offices have increased their use of alternative investments. In particular, hedge funds and funds of hedge funds now represent a much larger part of many portfolios due to their non-correlated nature and strong performance results. Almost three-quarters of family offices currently invest in hedge funds, with nearly 60 percent of this group planning additional allocations in the coming year.

Perhaps the biggest reason why family offices tend to outsource the selection, due diligence, and monitoring of hedge funds is because of a difficulty in hiring and retaining the proper personnel. These family offices realize that given the esoteric nature of the hedge funds, it is extremely important to outsource the selection process to a third party that has the necessary skill set. They also cite a lack of hedge fund investment transparency as a key concern along with lock-up periods, style drift, and fraud as other major concerns. As we saw in Chapter 1, "Recent Hedge Fund Scandals," a lot of high net worth individuals got taken in by relying too much on relationships and not hiring the appropriate advisors and consultants.

Banks

Perhaps the most natural and largest investors in hedge funds are banks. After all, just about every bank runs its own proprietary trading operation where it places bets on stocks, bonds, commodities, and so on. These proprietary desks utilize sophisticated strategies involving leverage, derivatives, and arbitrage models; they are, in most respects, small hedge funds inside banks. At some banks you will find several such mini hedge funds. The most successful proprietary traders from these banks then leave and either start their own hedge funds or join other hedge funds. Goldman Sachs is regarded as the world's largest and most successful investment bank. But it is also regarded as a giant hedge fund in disguise since close to 70 percent of its earnings in recent years have come from proprietary trading operations. Thus it is no surprise that quite a few hedge funds have been started by proprietary traders who have left Goldman Sachs in search of fame and fortune.

When a successful trader leaves a bank, he or she is generally "seeded" by that bank to start his or her own hedge fund. Seed deals provide investment capital to the departing trader in exchange for some economic benefit for the bank. A typical seed deal may involve the bank's giving the departing trader a $100 million in investment capital; in return, the bank would contract to pay only half of the typical 2 and 20 percent fees that the trader would charge when he or she sets up the new hedge fund. Sometimes banks would also retain a revenue sharing interest in the hedge fund.

Quite a few banks have set up their own internal fund of funds units to invest in hedge funds as well. These units generally fall under the bank's alternative asset management divisions. One would assume that given the talent the banks possess in terms of trading expertise, they would staff the alternative asset management units with senior traders from their proprietary trading units. But, given the way the economics are structured, most senior traders shy away from asset management assignments. This leaves the traditional asset manager with the task of investing in hedge funds. This is the core of the problem with the current hedge fund investing model that we will explore further in later chapters. As expected, improper due diligence on hedge funds performed by banks has recently landed them in hot water, as shown by the Madoff scandal. Following is a list of global banks that were invested in Madoff:

- **Banco Santander:** Spain's largest bank said its investment fund, Optimal, has a $3 billion exposure to Madoff Securities.
- **Fortis NV:** The Dutch banking unit of the group recently acquired by the Dutch government said it may have a loss of up to one billion euros due to loans made to funds that invested in Madoff Securities.

- **HSBC:** The banking and financial services group said it has potential exposure of $1 billion after providing financing to a small number of institutional clients who invested in funds with Madoff.
- **Benbassat & Cie:** The Swiss private bank has an exposure of $1 billion, according to Le Temps.
- **Natixis:** The French bank said it could have a 450 million euro indirect exposure to Madoff.
- **Royal Bank of Scotland:** The bank said it had exposure through trading and collateralized lending to funds of hedge funds invested with Madoff, with a potential loss of around 400 million pounds.
- **BNP Paribas:** France's largest listed bank said it has a potential 350 million euro exposure.
- **Dexia:** The Belgian bank said private banking clients had exposure to funds invested in Madoff of 78 million euros.
- **Nomura:** Japan's biggest brokerage firm said it had a $300 million exposure related to Madoff, but the impact on its capital would be limited.
- **Unicredit Spa:** The Italian bank said its own exposure to Madoff's alleged fraud is about 75 million euros. Some funds in its Pioneer Investments unit "are exposed to Madoff indirectly through feeder funds," it said.
- **UBI Banca:** The Italian bank said its exposure to Madoff amounted to 60 million euros.
- **Nordea Bank:** The Nordic region's biggest bank said its pension clients had an indirect exposure of 48 million euros to the alleged fraud.
- **Benedict Hentsch:** Swiss private bank said its exposure to products linked to Madoff amounted to $47 million, or less than 5 percent of assets under management.
- **Bank Medici:** The closely held Austrian bank serving wealthy clients and institutional investors said it held products affected by the fraud, but was not at risk in case of a loss. It declined to say how big the exposure was.
- **UBS:** The investment bank unit of the Swiss financial group said it has a limited and insignificant counterparty exposure.
- **Aozora Bank:** The Japanese bank said it had an estimated $137 million indirect exposure to Madoff through invested funds. It said it expected only limited impact on its capital.
- **BBVA:** Spain's second-largest bank said its international operation has about 30 million euros of exposure to Madoff, and it sees a maximum potential loss from Madoff-linked investments of 300 million euros.

Endowments

The category of endowments covers college and universities as well as charitable institutions. In the latest National Association of College and University Business Officers (NACUBO) Endowment Study, hedge funds have an allocation of 18 percent of college and university portfolios on a dollar-weighted basis. This puts hedge funds second to a 48 percent allocation in stocks. Fixed income investments, considered relatively safe, come in at third with only a 15 percent allocation. The rest of the allocation is generally held in cash and other miscellaneous categories. Additionally, the size of an institution also governs the percentage of assets invested in hedge funds. The larger the institution, the higher the percentage of assets invested in alternative investments such as hedge funds.

U.S. endowment funds are nontaxable vehicles established to contribute toward the future funding requirements of colleges and universities. The university endowments raise money from a combination of legacies, gifts, and government grants. They also rely on prudently deploying this capital to generate superior investment returns. In the United States there are over 750 endowments with an average of $520 million in funds, with the largest endowment fund at $35 billion for Harvard University. Overall, the U.S. endowment funds have achieved remarkable investment returns. This is especially the case for the largest endowment funds—those with assets greater than $10 billion dollars comprising Harvard, Yale, Stanford, Texas System, and Princeton. They have achieved an average ten-year annualized return of approximately 14.6 percent, roughly double the returns for traditional 50 percent equity and 50 percent bond portfolio, with significantly lower volatility. A look at the portfolios of the U.S. endowment funds shows exposure to multiple asset classes that provide additional diversification benefits. Once again, the largest endowment funds tend to be the leaders in portfolio innovativeness. Those endowment funds with assets greater than $10 billion hold roughly 57 percent of their portfolio in alternative assets, while the average U.S. endowment fund still holds roughly 80 percent in traditional assets. The additional diversification in large endowment portfolios is one of the reasons for their superior long-term investment performance. The two standouts in terms of U.S. university endowments are Harvard and Yale. Their investment return summary is provided in Table 2.1.

As per a report by the National Association of College and University Business Officers in Washington, D.C., U.S. college endowments on average have 8.6 percent of their assets in so-called alternative investments in 2008, which also include venture capital funds and private equity firms. That's up from 7.5 percent in 2007 and 6.8 percent in 2000. The average endowment rose 3 percent in the twelve months ended June 30, 2007, the first annual

TABLE 2.1   Summary of the Super Endowment Funds as of June 2007

Size ($bn)	2006 Annual Return	2007 Annual Return	10yr Annual Return	Investment Style
Harvard	34.90%	23.00%	15.00%	Diversified multi-asset
Yale	22.50%	28.00%	17.80%	Diversified multi-asset

Source: Annual reports (various)

gain since fiscal 2000, according to the association's study of over 700 endowments with combined assets of more than $230 billion. The returns were buoyed in part by hedge funds, which are the most popular alternative investment for colleges. Hedge funds now manage 6 percent of endowment assets, or more than $14 billion, which is up from 5 percent in 2006.

In a recent interview, the treasurer of University of Colorado, Judy Van Gorden, claimed that there was a continuing trend toward using hedge funds on the part of university endowments. "For a while, they were used mostly by big endowments. Now midsized and smaller endowments are looking to those as a way to reduce volatility and to diversify." The University of Colorado's $387 million endowment first invested about $40 million in hedge funds in 2001. The school now has $62 million, or 16 percent of assets, in hedge funds.

Besides university endowments, a lot of charitable foundations invest heavily in hedge funds as well to boost returns and use the income stream to pay for ongoing expenses. One only has to look at the recent Bernie Madoff scandal to see the charitable foundations that were invested with just one hedge fund and the losses they suffered. Following is a list of university endowments and charitable foundations that were invested with Bernie Madoff:

- **New York University:** Lost $24 million. This was invested into Madoff funds via Ezra Merkin's Ascot Partners funds of hedge funds.
- **Yeshiva University:** Lost $14.5 million. This was invested into Madoff funds via Ezra Merkin's Ascot Partners funds of hedge funds.
- **Chais Family Foundation:** This group, which donates about $12.5 million annually to Jewish causes, said it will be forced to close after the entire fund was invested with Madoff.
- **Boston Properties:** Chairman Mort Zuckerman told CNBC that about 10 percent of one of his charitable trusts was invested with Madoff and had lost about $30 million.

CONCLUSION

In this chapter, I have covered what are usually termed as the end-investors into hedge funds, that is, the pension funds, high net worth individuals (HNWs), banks, and endowments. These are large institutional investors that have billions of dollars to deploy and often define the investment trends of the future. It is quite obvious that these investors have recognized the importance of diversifying their return streams and also the need for excess market returns. They have also realized that hedge funds are such vehicles that can provide these diversified excess market returns.

But, identifying a course of action and implementing it successfully are two completely different processes. This chapter has also shown that improper due diligence by the so called hedge fund experts has led to catastrophic losses. Pension funds have lost billions and entire philanthropic foundations have been wiped out not just by outright Ponzi schemes but also by improper risk management by hedge funds. The need for professional advisors who have hands on experience as traders and risk managers has never been highlighted more than after a year like 2008. There are a lot of problems with the way the investors, retail as well as institutional, approach the process of hedge fund investing and in this book I have tried to outline these problems as well as propose solutions to these problems.

CHAPTER 3

Hedge Funds

Alfred Jones is credited with the creation of the first hedge fund in 1949. Jones believed that price movements of an individual asset could be seen as having a component due to the overall market, the systemic portion, and a component due to the performance of the asset itself, the idiosyncratic portion. In order to neutralize the effect of overall market movement, he balanced his portfolio by buying stocks whose price he expected to rise and selling short stocks he expected to fall. This helped in removing the systemic portion of the price movements, and he was left with the idiosyncratic performance of his long stock and short stock positions. This concept produced returns that were not market dependent and tended to hedge the market exposure to his portfolio. Thus was born the concept of a hedge fund and the principle of producing alpha or market independent returns.

As hedge funds are not required to register with any regulatory body like the SEC, it is hard to determine the actual number of hedge funds in existence. Hedge funds are operated from several countries around the world, but the majority of them are based in New York and Connecticut in the United States. In Asia, as the Chinese economy is starting to drive the market dynamics, we have seen Hong Kong and Singapore emerge as the two biggest hedge fund hubs. In Europe, London is considered the preferred location for hedge funds, especially hedge funds that trade in markets around the world. London's geographical location can be a big advantage for the hedge fund manager who is trying to keep an eye on market developments around the world in real time. When a trader walks into his or her office at 7 A.M. in London, it is 5 P.M. in Tokyo and 3 P.M. in Hong Kong. When a trader leaves his or her office at 6 P.M. in London, it is 1 P.M. in New York. This lets the London trader watch the closing of the Asian markets, trade in the Euro time zone and watch the activity in the U.S. market well into the afternoon. This gives him or her the opportunity to observe the market dynamics and follow the news from a truly global perspective.

TABLE 3.1 Single Manager Funds as of March 5, 2008

Name	AUM ($bn)
JP Morgan	$44.7
Farallon Capital	$36
Bridgewater Associates	$36
Renaissance Technologies	$34
Och-Ziff Capital Management	$33.2
Goldman Sachs Asset Management	$32.5
DE Shaw	$32.2
Paulson and Company	$29
Barclays Global Investors	$18.9
Man Investments	$18.8
ESL Investments	$17.5

Even though the hedge fund industry is managing $2 trillion across 9,400 hedge funds, the average hedge fund manages well under $100 million. There is a massive skew in the distribution because the bulk of the assets are managed by a handful of global hedge funds. Table 3.1 presents a list of the top hedge funds by assets under management.

Alfred Jones started his first hedge fund trading equities, where he would buy some stocks and sell short some other stocks. This strategy came to be known as Long/Short equity strategy. Since then the number of strategies and substrategies has expanded to cover all areas of the capital markets, including equities, fixed income, currencies, credit, commodities, and real estate. Furthermore, the approach taken in these markets varies from directional to relative value arbitrage. Before we delve deeper into each strategy and study how the hedge fund manager assesses opportunities and risks, it is worthwhile looking at the makeup of a hedge fund manager and the incentives offered for running a hedge fund.

INCENTIVES AND THE DISINCENTIVES OF THE HEDGE FUND FEE STRUCTURE

A typical hedge fund fee structure is 2 and 20 percent. A 2 percent annual management fee is supposed to pay for the salaries of the employees, office rent, Bloomberg, other data sources, and other operational expenses. In addition to this annual management fee, hedge funds charge a 20 percent performance fee on all profits generated by the hedge fund manager. Most successful traders decide to become hedge fund managers for the attraction of 20 percent performance fees, the source of the true riches for some of the most successful hedge fund managers, like George Soros, Steve Cohen, and Jim Simons. But the 2 percent management fee is not too shabby either, especially when you are managing vast sums of capital. For example, a fund that runs $1 billion in capital will collect $20 million in management fees every year. The operational expenses of running a hedge fund contain vast economies of scale, and soon enough a big portion of the management fees end up as incentive for the hedge fund manager for running larger and larger amounts of capital. The hedge fund fee structure has been a topic for hot debate because it can create the wrong incentives. On many occasions hedge fund managers have grown in size to a point that their core strategy cannot support the increased amounts of capital. As we saw in the case of Amaranth Capital, described in Chapter 1, the assets under management grew, and the convertible arbitrage strategy shrank in opportunity. This led Nick Maounis, the founder of Amaranth, to expand the scope of his strategy beyond his expertise, and he ended up allocating too much responsibility and capital to a 26-year-old trader, Brian Hunter. What happened to Amaranth and its investors' capital is history. Warren Buffett has also raised concerns over the 20 percent performance fees as he feels that it incentivizes the manager to take undue risk.

I feel that the problem with the hedge fund fee structure lies more with the management fees rather than the performance fees. The management fees should be a fixed dollar amount that the manager is allowed to charge the fund on an annual basis rather than a percentage of assets under management. This dollar amount should be the amount that is required to pay for the necessary operational expenses. The fund directors should be responsible for verifying the dollar amount of the annual management fees. This will ensure that the hedge fund manager's incentives are truly aligned with his or her investors'. The only way the hedge fund manager will make vast amounts of money for him- or herself is by making vast amounts of money for the investors. Then the hedge fund manager will only accept that amount of capital that he or she can prudently deploy in his or her strategy and not accept capital for the attraction of the management fees.

There is one caveat to this argument, though. The investor industry can mandate a floating management fee structure, but the free capital markets will let the successful hedge fund manager define his or her own fee structure. And that is fair, but what this new structure will do is to dissuade the charlatans and the substandard money managers from posing as hedge fund managers for the sake of the hefty management fees. As an example of the fee structure charged by some of the most successful managers, Steven

Cohen's SAC Capital Partners charges a 3 percent management fee and a 35 to 50 percent performance fee, while Jim Simons's Renaissance Technologies Corp. charged a 5 percent management fee and a 44 percent incentive fee in its flagship Medallion Fund. It can afford to; both have over 35 percent annualized net returns for several years running. *Trader Monthly*, a magazine dedicated to the hedge fund industry, produces a list of the top-paid hedge fund managers every year. Table 3.2 lists the compensation numbers of the top hedge fund managers for 2007.

Now that we understand the motivations for starting a hedge fund, let us explore the background, skill set, and the expertise of a typical hedge fund manager. The landscape is littered with traders, analysts, economists, bankers, and even mutual fund managers who have tried to roll the dice at the two and twenty casino. Most never get off the ground because they cannot find the necessary funding to launch their strategy. This could be because they do not have the necessary skill set or marketing expertise to sell their strategy, or worse, bad market timing, a year like 2008. From the small subset of hedge fund managers who do manage to launch their funds, most leave disappointed after the first year, slightly poorer but much wiser; some leave after a few years with a small fortune but too scarred to ever want to return to the battlefield; and a very small minority survive to become icons of the industry. According to hedge fund industry statistics, two

TABLE 3.2 Compensation of Top Hedge Fund Managers 2007

1	John Paulson, Paulson & Co.	$3 billion +
2	Philip Falcone, Harbinger Capital Partners	$1.5–$2 billion
3	Jim Simons, Renaissance Technologies	$1 billion
4	Steven A. Cohen, SAC Capital Advisors	$1 billion
5	Ken Griffin, Citadel Investment Group	$1 billion
6	Chris Hohn, The Children's Investment Fund Management (TCI)	$800–$900 million
7	Noam Gottesman, GLG Partners	$700–$800 million
8	Alan Howard, Brevan Howard Asset Management	$700–$800 million
9	Pierre Lagrange, GLG Partners	$700–$800 million
10	Paul Tudor Jones, Tudor Investment Corp.	$600–$700 million

Source: Trader Monthly

out of three hedge funds that actually manage to launch fail after the first three years.

EDUCATION OF THE FUTURE HEDGE FUND MANAGER

A hedge fund portfolio manager is a well-educated overachiever. If you were to look at the resume of a hedge fund manager, you would most likely find him educated at an Ivy League school. I purposefully say him, as the hedge fund industry is extremely male dominated. Lee Hennessee, founder of Hennessee Group, a New York firm that advises investors on choosing hedge funds, estimates management ranks in the hedge-fund industry are about 7 percent female, and that women may represent just 1 percent of the executives in the No. 1 or No. 2 spots. Most likely, the hedge fund manager proceeds to get an advanced degree in finance or economics at one of the leading graduate schools in the country. University of Pennsylvania's Wharton School of Business features quite prominently on the resumes of the hedge fund industry mavens. Even Bernie Madoff, who graduated from Hofstra University, wished he had attended Wharton or Stanford. I doubt that would have made any difference in his decisions down the road to commit the largest fraud in the financial history of the world. While most hedge fund managers would receive an MBA in Finance as an advanced degree, there are several managers with PhDs in physics, mathematics, and even medicine. The box illustrates educational profile of one of the most successful managers of the hedge fund industry who also has a nontypical education background.

Jim Simons, Renaissance Technologies (A $34 billion hedge fund)

Jim Simons received his bachelor's degree in mathematics and literature from the Massachusetts Institute of Technology in 1958, and his PhD, also in mathematics and literature, from the University of California at Berkeley in 1962 at the age of 23. From 1961 to 1964, he taught mathematics at Lancaster University. Between 1964 and 1968, he was on the research staff of the Communications Research Division of the Institute for Defense Analyses (IDA). In 1968, he was appointed chairman of the math department at Stony Brook (New York) University, transforming it into one of the top ten in the nation. In 1976, Simons won the American Mathematical Society's Oswald Veblen Prize in Geometry for work that involved a recasting of the subject of area minimizing multi-dimensional surfaces and characteristic forms. This resulted in his proof of the Bernstein conjecture up to real dimension 8 and an improvement of a certain "regularity" result of Wendell H. Fleming on a generalized plateaus problem. In 1978, he left academia to run an investment fund that traded in commodities and financial instruments on a discretionary basis.

TRAINING GROUNDS OF THE HEDGE FUND MANAGER

After graduating with a degree in finance from a school like Wharton or Chicago, the true vetting process of the future hedge fund manager begins. Most graduates land jobs on the trading desks of one of the major investment banks on Wall Street. Goldman Sachs is a name that comes up with very high frequency on the resumes of hedge fund managers. Goldman Sachs is regarded as the world's largest and most successful investment bank, but it is also regarded as a giant hedge fund in disguise because close to 70 percent of its earnings in recent years have come from proprietary trading operations. Therefore, it is no surprise that most graduates compete ferociously to get through the grueling seven- to eight-step interview process to secure a trading job at Goldman Sachs. It is considered one of the best training grounds for the future hedge fund manager.

A fresh graduate will spend anywhere from one to three years on the trading desk as an assistant trader. As an assistant trader, he or she will perform all the support functions for the head trader, who makes all the big trading calls on the desk. These support functions will include creating trading models, analyzing macro economic news, executing trades, booking the trades in internal systems, performing profit and loss reconciliations, and often fetching lunch for the boss as well. The assistant trader will often work longer hours than the head trader and will ingratiate himself so that the head trader can become his rabbi. In Judaism, *rabbi* means a religious teacher, or more literally, "my great one" when addressing any master. On a Wall Street trading desk a rabbi can be the difference between shown the door after three years or shown the path to success and untold riches. Most young graduates who start out on a trading desk have a life span of no more than three years. Either they decide that they do not have the requisite skill set and temperament to deal with the immense stress that comes with the job, or that decision is made for them by their superiors. A rabbi will guide his disciple and teach him trading skills that cannot be gleaned from any course at the business schools of Wharton or Chicago. Furthermore, a rabbi will protect his disciple from office politics and upheavals. Wall Street is constantly going through upheavals, some caused by the market conditions and some by the bank's own doing. During these periods of volatility, the trading desks either make a lot of money or lose a lot of money. When the losses come, heads need to roll. The only thing that keeps the young trader from being sacrificed at the altar of downsizing is his rabbi.

THE CHART READERS

During the first three years as an assistant trader, the apprentice acquires not just market analysis skills but more important, under the expert tutelage of his rabbi, he starts to develop acumen for the markets and his own trading style. Some traders become good at predicting market movements based on price data. They spend countless hours reading charts, drawing trend lines, and monitoring indicators like 100-day Moving Averages and Relative Strength Indices. Often the successful trader will develop his own system for predicting market movements. He might become a trend follower or a contrarian. He will look for technical signals from calculating some combination of price movements and volumes to determine the entry and exit points of a trade. One of the experts in the hedge fund industry at reading charts is Paul Tudor Jones, who founded the $10 billion Tudor Funds in 1986. In the interview with Jack Schwager for his book, *Market Wizards: Interviews with Top Traders*, Paul acknowledged that after testing several systems, he had found a trend following system that worked very well for him.

THE QUANTS

While some traders will become chart readers, others with a more quantitative bend might turn toward systematic trading. The science of predicting market price movements based on systems is termed *systematic trading*. Some hedge funds have stables of PhDs and computer scientists who have developed very complex algorithms for trading systems. Some of the biggest systematic trading hedge funds are AQR Capital Management, DE Shaw, and Renaissance Technologies. Each of these hedge funds has been founded by traders with quantitative academic and professional backgrounds. One of the co-founders of AQR Capital Management, which stands for Applied Quantitative Research, is Clifford Asness, PhD. Here is an excerpt from AQR's website's principal bios section, www.aqrcapital.com/cliff.htm, which states,

> Prior to co-founding AQR Capital Management, Cliff was at Goldman, Sachs & Co. where he was a Managing Director and Director of Quantitative Research for the Asset Management Division. Cliff

and his team at Goldman were responsible for building quantita-
tive models to add value in global equity, fixed income and cur-
rency markets for Goldman clients and partners. Cliff has authored
articles on many financial topics including multiple publications in
the Journal of Portfolio Management *and the* Financial Analysts
Journal. *Cliff received a BS in Economics from the Wharton School*
and a BS in Engineering from the Moore School of Electrical Engi-
neering, both graduating summa cum laude at the University of
Pennsylvania. He received an MBA with high honors and a PhD in
Finance from the University of Chicago.

Jim Simons, who runs Renaissance Technologies, does not even bother
hiring the Wall Street finance types. "We hire physicists, mathematicians,
astronomers, and computer scientists and they typically know nothing
about finance," Simons said in a keynote address at the International Association of Financial Engineers annual conference. "We haven't hired out of
Wall Street at all." His firm's scientists tap decades of diverse data in Renaissance's vast computer banks to assess statistical probabilities for the direction of securities prices in any given market. Experts attribute a breadth
of data and the firm's ability to manipulate it for its consistent success in
beating the markets.

The lesson for any hedge fund investor here is very simple. If some
hedge fund manager claims to have a trading system that can produce
steady returns year after year but does not have the requisite academic or
professional background to support his claims, be very skeptical. Both KL
Financial and Bernie Madoff claimed to possess secretive trading systems or
strategies that were complex and highly successful. Neither of the two
hedge fund managers possessed the necessary background to support their
claims. This should have been a very big red flag in any due diligence
process.

THE GLOBAL MACRO TRADER

Not all successful traders are chart readers or systematic traders; some trade
on market news and by analyzing global macroeconomic events. This approach is termed *global macro trading*, and one such very successful hedge
fund manager is George Soros, who has been an inspiration for several
young Wall Street traders to follow in his footsteps. George Soros was born
in Hungary in 1930 and escaped the Nazis to immigrate to England in
1947. He graduated from the London School of Economics in 1952 and
became a follower of the philosopher Karl Popper. In 1956 he moved to

New York City, where he worked as an arbitrage trader with F. M. Mayer and as an analyst with Wertheim and Company up to 1963. Throughout this time, Soros developed a philosophy of "reflexivity" based on the ideas of Karl Popper. Reflexivity, as used by Soros, is a set of ideas that seeks to explain the relationship between thought and reality, which he used to predict, among other things, the emergence of financial bubbles. Soros began to apply his theory to investing and concluded that he had more talent for trading than for philosophy. In 1973 he set up a private investment firm that eventually evolved into the Quantum Fund, one of the first hedge funds.

On Black Wednesday (September 16, 1992), Soros became famous when he sold short more than $10 billion worth of pounds, profiting from the Bank of England's reluctance to either raise its interest rates to levels comparable to those of other European Exchange Rate Mechanism countries or to float its currency. Finally, the Bank of England was forced to withdraw the currency from the European Exchange Rate Mechanism and to devalue the pound sterling, and Soros earned an estimated $1 billion in the process. He was dubbed "the man who broke the Bank of England."

FROM A CATERPILLAR TO A BUTTERFLY

All junior traders dream of being given their own capital to manage, so they can start to create an independent track record of their performance. Depending upon his or her skill level, success, and luck, a trader can land this assignment in two to three years after joining a trading desk. After managing capital successfully for a few years, the traders might find themselves running the trading desk and becoming a rabbi to some other aspiring trader. During this period, some traders might also leave a Wall Street bank and start trading for a hedge fund. So what makes a successful trader want to leave the comfort of earning a fat paycheck to want to become a hedge fund manager? It is usually the spirit of entrepreneurialism combined with the material desire to earn an even fatter paycheck. The usual compensation for a trader at a Wall Street bank or working for a hedge fund as a portfolio manager is between 8 and 15 percent of profits with a fixed base salary. The 2 and 20 fee structure of a hedge fund is the difference between chartering a private jet and owning a private jet with your hedge fund's name emblazoned on the side.

The time a trader spends on a trading desk at a Wall Street bank gives him or her the time to develop not just market analysis skills but also the discipline required to be a successful trader under all market conditions. The ability to trade with common sense and without emotions or ego often trumps pure academic or intelligence prowess. There is a saying on the world of trading, "The markets can stay irrational longer than you can stay solvent." At University of Chicago's Graduate School of Business, I was taught that the markets are efficient. All available information is readily priced into the markets and reflected in a security's price, therefore trading is futile and akin to gambling. If I had subscribed to this theory, I would never have entered the world of trading. What I learned was that over short periods of time, markets will be governed by pressures of supply and demand that can create short or long lasting trends. A market that trends in a particular direction for any period of time, by definition, is not an efficient market. That market is taking time to digest new information and slowly reflecting it in its price. This presents trading opportunities. A truly efficient market would instantly reflect the news in the security's price, thereby creating a jump in the price and not a trading opportunity (see Figures 3.1 and 3.2).

Skills of a Trader

It is only after those supply and demand pressures have abated that the market returns to some level of equilibrium. Trend-following traders would trade with the market direction caused by those supply and demand pressures, while the contrarian traders will look for a trade that benefits from the removal of those temporary pressures and an eventual reversion to some equilibrium price level. Both those traders would be correct in their approach, but the key to making money on the trade would be the entry and exit points. A trader's model might be completely accurate in picking

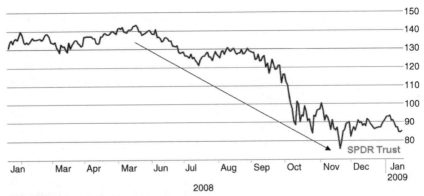

FIGURE 3.1 Example of a trending market.
Arrow shows the direction of the trend lasting over months.
Source: Charles Schwab, SPY Exchange Traded Fund

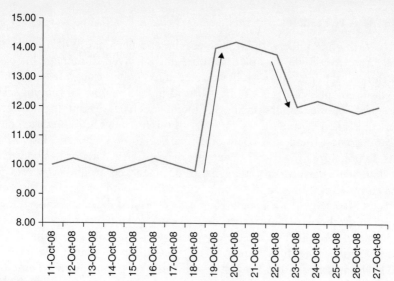

FIGURE 3.2 Example of an efficient market with price jump characteristics. Arrows show the price jump over a very short time periods.

the entry or exit point for the trade, but the market could keep trending in a particular direction longer than any model can predict. An egotistical trader would not set any stop loss levels, stay with the trade, and keep adding to his position until he ran out of capital or was stopped out of the trade by a higher power. Similarly, a less than confident trader would exit his position too soon or not have a big enough bet backing his conviction. In the world of trading, a lost trading opportunity is considered almost as bad as a losing trade. The successful trader learns how to size his trades correctly, how to pick stop loss and take profit levels, and is nimble. He does not let greed and fear make his trading decisions, and he does not freeze during moments of market panic. He never "bets the farm" on any one single trade and is constantly challenging and reexamining his own convictions. These trading disciplines cannot be imbibed in a classroom setting; they are only mastered in the heat of battle. And that is one reason why I firmly believe that no matter how talented an analyst, banker, or traditional mutual fund manager might be, he or she does not have the requisite skill set for being a successful trader over the course of time. Therefore, when performing due diligence on a hedge fund, every hedge fund investor should carefully look at the backgrounds of the trading personnel to make sure that at least some senior members possess the requisite trading skills.

Personality of a Trader

It is worthwhile understanding the psyche and personality of a trader as well. Any trader who has paid his dues and survived to manage his own portfolio and built a successful track record has gone through several bouts of elation, depression, self-doubt, frustration, and periods of humility. He has spent countless hours staring at Bloomberg charts, examining his Excel worksheet models, and skimming over a thousand news headlines each day. Most currency, bond, and commodity markets trade 24 hours a day. Markets do not care if the trader is sleeping, has a dinner date, or has to attend his daughter's play. Most traders that trade in markets around the world get woken up several times a night on a regular basis with telephone calls from brokers in different time zones. They have cancelled dates and missed their children's school performances due to sudden and unexpected market movements. A trader is direct, driven by logic, usually a person of few words, and has very little human interaction during the course of his workday. Often, a hedge fund investor will mistake a trader's demeanor for brusqueness and lack of social graces and decide to invest with a hedge fund manager who is more eloquent and sociable. They forget that there is no correlation—or perhaps even a negative one—between a trader's ability to effectively trade capital and his social skills.

Life as a hedge fund manager takes its toll on the trader's life. There is a saying on Wall Street that "traders age like dogs," that is, they age by seven years for every year that passes by. Some of my friends would argue that they almost aged a lifetime in a year like 2008. The career lifespan of a trader is short, and there is no exception for a hedge fund trader, either. I would like to end this chapter by discussing a letter written by one such hedge fund manager who left the battlefield in 2008, Andrew Lahde. He was no icon of the industry, so I doubt many have heard of him, but the letter was quite telling of the pressures of running a hedge fund, especially in a market climate like 2008.

ANDREW LAHDE'S GOODBYE LETTER

Andrew Lahde ran a relatively small hedge fund, with roughly $80 million in capital, called Lahde Capital Management, out of Santa Monica, California. He earned considerable fame when he racked up 1000 percent returns in 2007 betting correctly on the subprime crisis. But, what gained Andrew Lahde global recognition was not the massive returns he generated for his investors, but the fact that he decided to leave the industry at his peak and bow out in style. In 2008, he turned off his Bloomberg terminals for the last time, returned his investor's capital and turned his back to the world of hedge fund trading for good.

In October 2008, he sent an open goodbye letter to his investors where he commented on the cause of the credit crisis and what enabled him to generate 1000 percent returns. He called upon the rich and famous of the industry to help save American capitalism and ended his letter extolling the virtues of hemp and marijuana. The letter was a compelling read and I have outlined some sections from his letter in the following paragraphs.

Andrew Lahde's letter outlined the sheer incompetence of the supposedly well-educated executives who helped fuel the credit boom that eventually led to the credit crisis of 2007. "The low hanging fruit, i.e., idiots whose parents paid for prep school, Yale, and then the Harvard MBA, was there for the taking." He called these executives, traders and legislators unworthy of the education they supposedly received, and stated that their shoddy decisions were directly responsible for the bankruptcy of storied Wall Street institutions, such as AIG, Bear Stearns, and Lehman Brothers. Andrew further remarked, "All of this behavior supporting the Aristocracy, only ended up making it easier for me to find people stupid enough to take the other side of my trades."

Andrew's letter was also telling of the pressures of running a hedge fund; the personal sacrifices, the constant uphill battle to raise capital, often against other managers with bigger reputations and financial backings of rich friends and family. Andrew stated that his main objective for becoming a hedge fund trader was purely financial; a claim in my opinion, that would be supported by close to 99 percent of the current and prospective hedge fund managers in the industry. Andrew said that he was very happy walking away from the industry with a relatively small fortune. He sympathized with the stressful lives of the harried hedge fund managers and called their struggle to amass large fortunes an aimless pursuit. While referring to these managers, Andrew Lahde wrote, "Appointments back to back, booked solid for the next three months, they look forward to their two week vacation in January during which they will likely be glued to their Blackberries or other such devices. What is the point? They will all be forgotten in 50 years anyway." As a personal note, I could not agree more with Andrew on this point.

Further along in his letter, Andrew also touched upon one of my favorite subjects, the lamentable trend we have seen in the government over the last few decades where the legislators seem to have lost the principles of capitalism laid down by our forefathers. The legislators of late have forgotten the basic precepts of capitalism and have been driven by lobbyists and politics. In his letter, Andrew stated, "First, I point out the obvious flaws, whereby legislation was repeatedly brought forth to Congress over the past eight years, which would have reigned in the predatory lending practices of now mostly defunct institutions." Andrew further calls upon the mavens of the hedge fund industry, like George Soros, who have the wealth as well as the clout, to sponsor forums to save American capitalism from further erosion due to corruption.

Lahde ended his letter pointing out the usefulness of hemp for the past 5,000 years as an alternative source of food and energy. He claimed that hemp could be a way of self-sufficiency for America's food and energy needs in the future. He further made an applaudable point on the benefits of marijuana as well, "The evil female plant—marijuana. It gets you high, it makes you laugh, it does not produce a hangover. Unlike alcohol, it does not result in bar fights or wife beating." Lahde claimed that the only reason marijuana remains illegal in the United States is because Corporate America has economic interests to sell expensive and addictive drugs like Paxil, Zoloft, Xanax, and through powerful lobbying has influenced legislation in their favor.

CHAPTER 4

Hedge Fund Strategies

Now that we have examined the world of trading and the evolution of a trader, taking him from a trading desk to a hedge fund, I would like to introduce the reader to some of the more popular hedge fund trading strategies. Along with the description of these strategies, I have also tried to offer some insight into the different skill sets required for executing each strategy. I am sure investors have wondered how a Long-Short equity hedge fund manager like Steve Cohen compares with Warren Buffett, the sage of Omaha and widely regarded as the savviest stock picker of our time. This chapter addresses the difference between a long-term investor like Buffett and a trader like Steve Cohen. I end the chapter with an insight into how these strategies performed in 2008 and the market climate for these strategies going forward.

The hedge funds will operate in any and every asset class imaginable, from the traditional equities and bonds to currencies, commodities, real estate, and even fine art. The geographical focus of these strategies includes the world. While most of the strategies are concentrated in the G10 or the developed countries, there are several funds focused on the emerging markets of Asia, Latin America, and Eastern Europe. We are also seeing hedge funds foray into the so-called frontier markets, or the extremely underdeveloped markets, of Africa and the Middle East. Even the instruments used by the hedge funds are diverse. Besides the traditional stock and bond holdings, hedge funds utilize derivative instruments such as futures, swaps, and options very heavily. Derivative instruments provide additional liquidity, leverage, and anonymity and can help focus the strategies. In fact, there are some strategies that exclusively use only derivative instruments, like Relative Value Arbitrage.

The pie chart in Figure 4.1 shows the approximate breakdown of hedge fund assets by strategy.

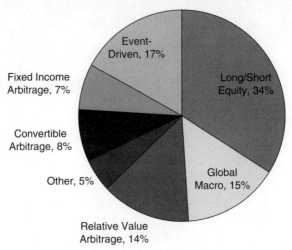

FIGURE 4.1 Breakdown of assets by strategy.
Source: HFR—PerTrac

LONG-SHORT EQUITY

As described earlier, a long-short equity strategy entails buying stocks that are cheap and selling short stocks that are expensive. A measure of a stock's valuation can be ascertained from various data metrics, such as price/earnings or price/book ratios. A successful long-short equity manager looks at several things about a company than just these typical ratios. The long-short equity hedge fund manager has to worry about macro economic events as well as company-specific news. Even though a long-short portfolio is supposed to hedge out all market-specific risk, rarely do we find managers not taking at least some market-directional view in their portfolio. Such portfolios might have 60 percent long stocks and 40 percent short stocks, thereby producing a 20 percent long bias. Sometimes the long portfolio might be in a sector that is correlated to commodity prices, while the short portfolio might be more interest rate sensitive, thereby creating macroeconomic risk. Even if the portfolio is constructed to be market neutral, the manager is glued to the newswires during the trading hours for company-specific news events, which can range from management shakeups, product releases, news about competitors, and of course, scandals. Often, detailed due diligence is performed on stocks by equity analysts at investment banks, but most times hedge funds have their own stable of equity analysts to fill this role. Equity analysts produce reports and issue upgrades or downgrades on stocks that can be big price movers. The biggest long-short equity managers

TABLE 4.1 Comparing Warren Buffett, Steve Cohen, and S&P 500 Returns from 1998–2008

Market	Average Annual Returns
S&P 500	−0.70%
Berkshire Hathaway (Class B shares)	7.0%
SAC Capital Management	32%

that pay the largest fees to investment banks always vie to be the first to get hints on these upcoming analyst reports, before they are released to the general marketplace.

One might wonder what separates a Warren Buffett, the sage of Omaha and well known as the best stock picker of our time, from a Steve Cohen, the best regarded long-short equity hedge fund manager. Warren Buffett is a value investor. He buys and holds companies that are cheap from a valuation perspective and holds them for years, riding the bull and bear cycles. Steve Cohen is a trader. He rarely buys and holds a stock for years and will often trade it several times over the course of a year, going both long and short. A trader will try to make money from the several up and down moves, thereby attempting to generate a much larger return. This exercise is called generating alpha generation or producing market excess returns and can be seen when comparing Berkshire Hathaway share performance to SAC Capital Management's returns. The data in Table 4.1 covers from January 1998 to December 2008 and is reported after deducting the hefty fees charged by SAC Capital.

Even in a year like 2008, SAC Capital International Ltd, Steve Cohen's oldest and best performing fund, was down only 5.5 percent while the S&P 500 was down 37 percent and Berkshire Hathaway's B shares were down 28 percent. But, every long-short equity hedge fund manager is not a Steve Cohen, and that is reflected in the sector's returns of 8.5 percent annualized over the last twelve years compared to SAC's 32 percent over the same time period.

EVENT DRIVEN

Event-driven strategies also focus on the equity markets and individual companies. An event-driven investment manager is typically looking to invest in situations where there is some form of corporate activity or impending change taking place. Corporate activity can include mergers and takeovers, restructuring, reorganizations, spin-offs, asset sales, liquidations, bankruptcy, and many others. Such corporate events can create wild swings in stock prices as information is hard to come by and the market is constantly trying to price in news as well as rumors. This type of event is a perfect example of an inefficient market because even in developed markets, the news is not readily available. Hedge fund managers that specialize in this area tend to rely heavily on strong knowledge-based or sophisticated models of corporate events and reliable sources of deal as well as company-specific research.

Merger or risk arbitrage is probably the most commonly known event-driven investment strategy. Let us take a simple example: U.S. company "A" is subject to a cash takeover at $50 a share by another U.S.–based company. Prior to the deal announcement, the company "A" share price was $30 per share. After the deal is announced, company A's shares trade at $45 a share. The reason why there is usually a gap left between the trading price and the buyout price is because buyout deals are generally subject to a number of conditions including financing, shareholder approval, and regulatory clearance and can take months to close. As several deals get put on hold or run into obstacles, the $5 discount reflects these risk factors. But, for an event-driven hedge fund manager, this $5 reflects a money-making opportunity, as this could be a 22.20 percent return on capital if the deal closes:

$$\$5/\$45 \times 12 \text{ months}/6 \text{ months} = 22.20\%$$

Another potential positive factor that the event-driven hedge fund manager considers is that a second bidder could emerge, thereby creating a price war and driving the stock price even higher. Besides the risks mentioned above, if the deal is complex—for example, a stock swap—the risks can increase. The event-driven hedge fund manager relies on his news network throughout the merger acquisition industry to create an advantage for himself. Some other types of event driven strategies are as follows:

Capital structure arbitrage: This involves taking long and short positions in the same company—for example, buying the debt versus shorting the stock in anticipation of a rights issue or long senior debt versus short junior debt in anticipation of a debt restructuring or bankruptcy that would favor the senior debt holders.

Distressed Debt: This involves buying debt of distressed companies. These companies may be experiencing severe operating or financial difficulties or even have started the process of restructuring through the sale of assets, a debt-for-equity swap, or a filing for bankruptcy.

The event-driven investment manager is seeking to identify situations where he believes the market is undervaluing the potential returns to the bondholder of a successful restructuring, a sale, or a liquidation of the company.

As can be seen from the above examples of event-driven strategies, the skill set required by the hedge fund manager is quite different from that of the long-short manager or the global macro manager. The skill set requires a deep knowledge of the investment banking industry and a robust Rolodex of industry contacts. Some event-driven investment managers screen a large universe of risk-arbitrage deals and rely largely on market-driven probability models to identify attractive investment opportunities while others perform detailed and extensive analysis of the companies involved, including the rationale, nature, and terms of the transactions, legal, competition, and regulatory issues before making investment decisions.

GLOBAL MACRO

As the strategy name implies, global macro entails a global, top-down analysis of the macroeconomic conditions. The manager will look at economic data, such as GDP, inflation, and trade and also analyze the Central bank's monetary policies and the government's fiscal policies. Besides economic data, the global macro manager will also look at geopolitical events. Changes in governments, wars and other political strife, trade, and currency protectionism can all play major roles in providing trading direction. As can be seen in the press over the last few years, the pressure exerted on China by the U.S. Senate forced China to end its currency peg and let its currency strengthen versus the U.S. dollar. While some global macro hedge fund managers will establish positions based on macroeconomic analysis only, most others will undertake several other steps of analysis. Some of the more popular secondary and tertiary levels of analysis include relative value or systematic analysis.

Relative Value Analysis refers to analyzing the markets in greater depth by studying interest rate yield curves, volatility cubes, and correlations between related markets and securities to determine cheapness. This analysis almost exclusively involves derivative instruments like options, futures, and swaps. A trader might determine that instead of buying two-year bonds on anticipation of interest rate cuts in the monetary policy of a country, the risk reward was better captured by buying two-year bonds and selling ten-year bonds at the same time. This trader might even establish the same view through a combination of options on the two-year and ten-year bonds.

Relative Value Analysis lets the global macro trader capture the cheapness that might emerge from certain supply and demand flows in the market.

The art of predicting market price movements based on systems is termed Systematic Trading. It is highly mathematical and the trading decisions are made by computer-based algorithms rather than human intervention. There are some managers who rely solely on systematic trading such as AQR Capital, DE Shaw and Renaissance Technologies, as mentioned earlier. Most likely, a global macro hedge fund manager may employ pieces of a systematic macro strategy to assist in his analysis rather than rely solely on a black-box to determine market moves. The manager may use the signals coming out of his systematic model to act as a second filter for his macroeconomic analysis, or he may use the signals to determine the best entry and exit points in a strategy. Sometimes the systematic portion of a global macro strategy might simply be looking at charts and drawing trend lines or looking at 100-day moving averages and relative strength indices (RSI).

A true global macro manager will invest across a range of markets, including fixed income, equity, currency, and commodities as well as geographies. There are a lot of specialized macro strategies as well that might focus solely on the developed G10 markets, emerging markets, or a specific region, such as Asia focused. The instruments used by the global macro manager are varied as well. While some will buy bonds, most markets can only be accessed efficiently through derivative instruments like futures, swaps, and options. A global macro manager who extensively uses derivative instruments has to be very adept at managing risk that comes with the use of derivative instruments. Therefore, it is quite common to see global macro managers assisted by risk managers who have Ph.D.s and are experts in measuring leverage and nonlinear risks that arise from derivative securities. I will discuss such risks and the appropriate due diligence measures needed for a derivative securities portfolio in Chapter 8.

FIXED-INCOME ARBITRAGE

Income arbitrage strategy refers to exploiting pricing inefficiencies between related fixed-income securities. Fixed-income securities refer to all types of bonds. These can be sovereign bonds issued by governments, government agencies, or corporations. The term *arbitrage* often carries the connotation of a risk-free transaction where one attempts to profit by exploiting price differences of identical or similar financial instruments on different markets or in different forms.

A popular fixed-income arbitrage strategy has been buying or selling government bonds and hedging with bond futures contracts while looking for price convergence between the two. Fixed-income arbitrage hedge funds look for price discrepancies across the spectrum of instruments like bonds, swaps, and futures. Often these price discrepancies are very small, and for to generate a substantial profit the manager utilizes leverage of as much as 20 to 25 times the capital. Leverage can cut both ways—it can magnify profits as well as losses. Borrowed capital can become expensive, and lenders may even reduce credit lines, thereby leading to forced position liquidation. As mentioned earlier, "markets can stay irrational longer than a hedge fund manager can stay solvent," and this can lead to small price discrepancies becoming larger, thus leading to massive losses in the portfolios.

Perhaps the best example of a fixed-income arbitrage hedge fund that got itself into overleveraged positions and ended up losing all of its client's capital was Long Term Capital Management, run by a group of highly talented and experienced managers. There is an entire book dedicated to this mess by Roger Lowenstein titled *When Genius Failed*.

Proper risk management techniques include measuring the amount of leverage, depth of the market, and market positioning; these techniques are extremely important in considering a fixed-income arbitrage strategy. The advent of technology, globalization of the markets, and the sophistication of the trading desks has removed most of these price discrepancies in the fixed-income arbitrage markets or made this strategy not as riskless as it implies. Wall Street and hedge fund desks have hired some of the brightest mathematicians and physicists to develop models that ensure that riskless trading opportunities are few and far between. This has forced a lot of the fixed-income arbitrage hedge funds to become more relative value-type funds where they take some level of view on the market direction.

RELATIVE VALUE ARBITRAGE

Relative value arbitrage strategy is very similar to fixed-income arbitrage in terms of analysis and construction, except it is not a riskless transaction. The relative value hedge fund manager takes a directional view on the movement of interest rates, monetary policy, credit spreads, or volatility. The strategy is mathematical in nature but does not rely on a computer-based algorithm like the systematic macro strategy does. The relative value hedge fund manager will analyze yield curves, volatility cubes, correlation matrices, and historical spreads between securities to determine cheap or expensive securities. He will then take a long position in the cheap security and a short position in the expensive security. He is betting that the short-term dislocation in prices is a manifestation of the supply and demand flows and that the market will soon return to some level of equilibrium. He is often also taking an underlying directional view on the markets as part of the market correction.

Following are some of the subsets of the relative value arbitrage strategy:

Yield Curve Relative Value: Relative value between government bonds of different maturities.

Equity Market Neutral: Relative value between stocks of two companies in the same sector.

Convertible Arbitrage: Relative value between the stock and the embedded value of the stock option in the company's convertible bond.

Credit Long-Short: Relative value between different bonds of a country, government agency, or a company

The above-described strategies are some of the more popular strategies employed by the hedge fund managers, but not an exhaustive set by any means. As the markets evolve, new money-making opportunities constantly keep presenting themselves while some other strategies might start to die out. Hedge fund managers keep incorporating new strategies into their trading universe while trying to weed out the ones that might have seen their best days. Given the cyclical nature of markets, it is very likely that certain strategies that might become unpopular today might come back into the mainstream again in a few years.

As can be seen from the above-described strategies, the skill set required to effectively manage capital in each strategy is quite different. It takes years

TABLE 4.2 Hedge Fund Returns Compared to S&P 500 Returns

	Annualized 12 yrs: January 1997–December 2008	2008
HFRI Equity Hedge Index	8.48%	−26.16%
HFRI Event Driven Index	8.33%	−21.26%
HFRI Macro Index	8.43%	5.18%
HFRI Convertible Arbitrage Index	−0.05%	−58.37%
HFRI Relative Value Arbitrage Index	6.72%	−16.77%
HFRI Merger Arbitrage Index	7.53%	−4.62%
S&P 500	3.21%	−37.00%

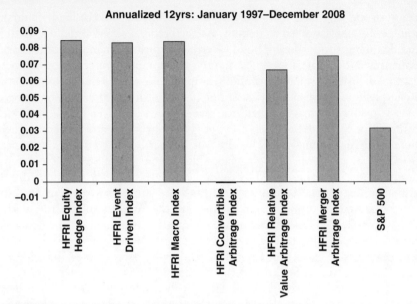

FIGURE 4.2 Annualized 12 yrs: January 1997–December 2008.

of specific education, especially for some of the more quantitative strategies like systematic macro and relative value, followed by years of practical experience on a trading desk to master the craft. Nearly every major hedge fund has senior traders who have the requisite pedigrees. None of them were day traders who quit their regular jobs and became successful hedge fund managers. This is an important point to remember for the investor when he or she is performing due diligence on a hedge fund manager.

Table 4.2 and Figure 4.2 compare the returns of the different hedge fund strategies and that of the S&P 500 over the last 12 years. Nearly every hedge fund strategy outperformed the S&P 500, even in a year like 2008, except convertible arbitrage.

EFFECT OF 2008 ON THESE STRATEGIES AND LOOKING FORWARD

The market environment of 2008 proved to be a graveyard for most hedge fund strategies. While most of them beat the S&P500s dismal performance of −37 percent, all, save one, failed to deliver the purported absolute returns that an investor expects from a hedge fund strategy. The growth in the global economies that had been funded by the flow of easy and cheap credit of the past four years came to a screeching halt as the high-yielding, low-credit assets started to default. As the credit markets dried up, so did the financing for corporate bond offerings and the demand for new stock issuances. No sector of the stock market was immune from capital outflows as a mad rush for safety of capital trumped all logic of relative valuations. Relationships between asset classes or bonds of different credits or maturities or currencies that had held for several years and even decades started to break down as the markets were governed by panic and hysteria rather than fundamental analysis. This fire was further fueled by a an admittance of failure by the credit rating agencies like Moody's and S&P, thereby rendering credit ratings assigned by them meaningless. Throw on top of this a global failure of the banking system and the subsequent bailout, and in some cases part nationalization, of some of the largest banks in the world like Citibank, AIG, and RBS, and we had what was termed by the media as "the worst economic recession since the Great Depression of 1929." This led to a massive exodus of capital from all risky asset classes and geographies back into the safe haven of U.S. Treasury bonds.

Hedge fund strategies like relative value arbitrage, convertible and fixed-income arbitrage rely very heavily on the past relationships between various bonds and their derivative instruments to hold into the future. But, in 2008 these decade-long relationships broke down, and therefore the hedge fund strategies that relied on mean reversion of these relationships performed the worst. Most equity-based hedge fund strategies are supposed to generate returns by taking no directional view on the markets (long-short type strategies) or by taking short-term views on market direction by going both long and short.

As Warren Buffett has stated many times, "it is only when the tide goes down that we find out who has been swimming naked." In 2008 we found out that most equity-based hedge fund strategies were closet long-only strategies that had been riding the bull market wave of the last few years. The one strategy that did perform well was the global macro strategy. Quite a few hedge fund managers in this space were able to spot the dark clouds in the horizon and thereby establish positions that would benefit from monetary and fiscal intervention by the Central banks around the world to shore up their economies.

I wish I could tell the reader which hedge fund strategies will make money in the next two to three years and which strategies to avoid. One thing is certain: Days of easy credit, low volatility, and trending markets are behind us for a while. It is not the hedge fund strategy but the hedge fund trader that generates returns (a topic of detailed discussion in my later chapters). If I had to pick one class of hedge funds, I would say that the investors should pick pure traders who are willing to take short-term positions and are nimble in their approach. The hedge fund industry was created to give investors an opportunity to invest with professional traders, not long-term money managers. We already have thousands of mutual funds that provide investment vehicles for investors who are interested in long-term directional exposure to the markets. Over the course of the last five to seven years, as the hedge fund industry has ballooned, this distinction between a trader and a long-term money manager has been lost. With over 7,000 hedge funds, it has become hard for the hedge fund investor to distinguish between a true alpha-generating trader and a closet beta (market directional) manager. One thing is for certain, the hedge fund industry does not have 7,000 top class traders running their own hedge funds; I would put that number closer to 100. Additionally, that exclusive 100 list is not a constant; its members keep changing with market conditions, managers' personal wealth and motivations, and new entrants with new technology and new ideas. What I have provided in my later chapters are tools for the hedge fund investors, retail as well as institutional, to help identify some of this top talent and avoid the sub-standard managers as well as the outright charlatans.

CHAPTER 5

Hedge Fund Service Providers and Regulators

To become a successful hedge fund manager requires more than just the requisite education and experience. It requires perseverance and luck to survive the crucial first three years and reach a critical mass in terms of assets under management, or AUM as is widely referred to in the industry. The critical mass can be the difference between surviving a bad period of drawdowns and shutting down the fund. Critical mass is a number that keeps increasing with the size of the industry. When I launched my hedge fund in 2004, critical mass was considered to be around $100 million, but now in 2009 it is more like $500 million. To understand the importance of critical mass, we have to look at how a typical hedge fund manager starts out of the gate. A typical hedge fund manager will usually start out with $25 million to $50 million. He will use his own savings—minimum amount is usually $1 million—raise capital from friends and family, as well as from his previous employer. As most hedge fund managers had successful trading careers at banks before they left to start their own hedge funds, they usually get seeded by their banks. The banks will provide the startup capital of anywhere from $50 million to $500 million dollars in exchange for favors like fee concessions, capacity, or prime brokerage business.

BUILDING A BUSINESS

Some hedge fund managers are unable to raise enough capital from their previous employers or through the usual friends and family network. These managers have the choice of starting with a very small amount of capital or approaching one of the several commercial seeders. A seeder will provide the aspiring hedge fund manager with startup operating capital as well as trading capital. In return, the seeder will assume a certain percentage ownership stake in the hedge fund. The usual seed investment provided by these commercial seeders is in the tune of $25 to $50 million. At launch, a hedge fund manager's investor base might be made up of a commercial seed investor, previous employer, or a small group of friends and family members. Needless to say, the investor base is shaky, and the assets are too small to eke out a satisfactory lifestyle after paying all the expenses. Therefore, the hedge fund manager's goal is to produce outstanding returns with low risk, so he can market his fund to the next stage of investors, the funds of hedge funds.

The funds of hedge funds carry a bad reputation. They have been blamed for not understanding the strategies that they invest in and being solely driven by backward looking performance numbers. At the first sign of drawdowns, the funds of funds can redeem their investment, which can lead to the demise of the hedge fund. But they are a necessary step in helping the manager get to a critical mass. The critical mass varies based on the strategy deployed, but in the current environment, as mentioned earlier, it is considered to be around $500 million. Once the hedge fund has reached the critical mass, he can start marketing directly to the institutional investors, like pension funds, endowments, and banks. Institutional investors invest large amounts of capital and are considered more stable than the funds of hedge funds.

The success of a hedge fund is defined not just by the expertise of the manager but also by his ability to pick the appropriate service providers. A hedge fund manager has to decide on a law firm to draw up his legal documents, an auditor to audit his fund's performance numbers, an administrator, a custodian, prime brokers, and fund marketers. Much has been written in other books on how to setup a hedge fund, and these books cover in greater detail the roles and functions of the service providers. I would like to approach the service providers' roles from an investor due diligence perspective.

When the industry and the hedge fund manager are performing well, little attention gets paid to the type and level of due diligence a service provider performs. It is only in difficult times of poor performance and scandals that finger-pointing starts. An investor should understand what level of due diligence to expect from the service providers and what level of due diligence he or she has to perform on a hedge fund manager, so there is little confusion in times of trouble. Therefore, along with a description of the services, each of the following sections also outlines important pitfalls that are not very obvious that an investor should be aware of.

Lawyers

A fund manager hires a reputable legal firm to help in setting up the hedge fund legal structure; complying with securities and derivatives regulatory matters; drafting operating agreements, marketing arrangements, trading documentation, exchange listing, Internet usage; and handling tax and ERISA matters. Due to tax regulations and to allow non-U.S.–based investors to invest in the fund, the fund is generally set up in a independent tax haven like the Cayman Islands, British Virgin Islands, or Bermuda. There is no office space with employees in any of these islands that advertise the presence of the hedge fund. The fund exists in a ledger of the offshore administrator of the fund. The offshore administrator's responsibility is to pay the registration fees and submit annual reports to make sure that the fund is in good standing with the offshore authorities. All trading operations of the fund are handled by the management company. The management company could be based in New York, Greenwich, London, or wherever the hedge fund manager decides to trade.

The Offering Memorandum: Caveat Emptor

The fund manager hires the legal firm and therefore the legal firm is there to watch out for the hedge fund manager's interests and not the investors'. The most important document that the investor needs to study and have his or her own lawyer read is the Offering Memorandum (OM). The OM lists the hedge fund manager's background, the fund's strategy, the fee structure, redemption restrictions, and risk disclosures. All these need to be looked at very carefully. The fund manager's background should list his education and trading experience along with details of the schools he attended, previous employers, and dates. As I have shown earlier, it takes specific education and experience to become a profitable hedge fund manager. The OM will outline whether the manager and his team possess the necessary skills.

Strategy and Risk Section   The fund's strategy and risk section is also very important. The strategy section should provide details on the markets that the manager will trade as well as the deployment of your investment dollars. It is important to look out for exceptions, like side pockets. Usually the lawyers will draft the OM in a way that gives the manager flexibility to stray from the stated strategy. Often this is innocuous and there to protect the manager, but sometimes you might think that you are invested in a long-short equity strategy and find that the manager is moonlighting as a currency trader as well.

Risk and strategy go hand in hand. The risk disclosure section will outline all the risk factors that the strategy and the investor are exposed to. Investors should not count on getting any level of detailed risk picture from the OM. The OM will list pretty much every single market segment the strategy could be exposed to and every possible risk event that could cause the investor to lose 100 percent of his or her investment. And that is the key. Despite all assurances from the fund manager, the investor has to assume that he or she could lose 100 percent of his or her investment. It happened in the case of Madoff, which was a fraud, and in the case of Long Term Capital Management where the fund was overleveraged. It will happen again. The best protection an investor can have is expert ongoing due diligence on the hedge fund managers to ensure that the risk controls are being followed and the investor's interests are being protected.

Fees and Redemption Section   The fees and redemption section outlines the direct fee structure that the management company will charge the fund as well as the expenses that will be passed to the fund. The management company will usually charge an annual management fee, a performance fee based on profits. It also might have an upfront sales fee and an early redemption fee as well. Besides the fees, the fund shareholders will also be responsible for certain fund-related expenses. The customary charges are fund auditing, legal, and administrator-related expenses, but the fund managers have been known to pass on research, travel, and even employee salaries to the fund. The fee section will disclose all those charges. The redemption section is very important to understand because it will explain how the investor can have access to his or her funds. Depending upon the strategy, the funds will allow redemption on a monthly, quarterly, or annual basis. If the strategy has been marketed as a liquid strategy, then the redemption terms should be commensurate with it as well. As a lot of investors found out in 2008, there is usually an overriding clause in the OM regarding redemptions that few investors care to read and understand. This is the "gate" clause. The gate clause effectively lets the fund manager suspend or limit redemptions to "safeguard the investor's interests." The investors have been shocked to see some of the biggest and oldest hedge funds like Tudor, Citadel, and others suspend redemptions for one to two years in their main funds. Sometimes the fund will suspend redemptions in a volatile and illiquid market to avoid selling at fire sale prices, which would benefit neither the fund manager nor his investors. Often the gate clause is for the protection of the manager rather than the investors. By erecting the gate, the fund manager protects the assets under management and hopes that as the market conditions improve, the investors would change their minds and not redeem their capital. It is a perfectly legal and rational approach from the manager's perspective, but it does the investor no good, especially if he or she did not understand the gate clause and was counting on getting their capital back.

The information in the OM takes precedence over any other discussion or marketing material that the investor might have been provided with. The investor has to perform his or her own due diligence at the onset and then continue with it on an ongoing basis just as if he or she was invested in a publicly traded stock. Complexity of a hedge fund's strategy and the lack of transparency make this difficult; therefore, employing experts in the field of trading and risk management is paramount. Following is the overall ranking of the law firms as per Institutional Investor's Alpha Magazine 2007 Awards:

U.S.-Based Law Firms

Ranking	Law Firm
1	Sidley Austin
2	Shartsis Friese
3	Seward & Kissel

Offshore-Based Law Firms

Ranking	Law Firm
1	Ogier
2	Maples and Calder
3	Walkers

Administrators and Custodians

Hedge funds hire independent administrators and custodians to provide the investors with a sense of security that their capital is being accounted for by a third party. A fund administrator provides the back office services required in running a hedge fund. A typical administrator will provide the following fund accounting services:

- Preparing fund's financial statements, including Balance Sheets, Income Statements, Partners' Capital Allocation Schedules, and Fund Performance Schedules
- Preparing of Investor Account Statements
- Recording expenses and capital transactions in accordance with U.S. GAAP and fund-governing documents (including accruals, subscriptions, and redemptions)
- Reconciling cash accounts with statements provided by prime brokers or custodians
- Maintaining a record of each investor's capital balance and allocating profits and losses in accordance with the partnership agreement
- Maintaining documentation of subscription and redemption notices
- Calculating management fee and incentive allocation/carried interest based on the fund's governing documents

- Performing investor due diligence in compliance with U.S. Patriot Act Requirements
- Providing the fund's tax advisor with accounting records to assist in the preparation of the fund's annual income tax returns
- Providing necessary accounting records to the auditor for the fund's annual audit

The abovementioned tasks are required to be performed by any hedge fund. But given the complexity of these tasks and the required expertise, investment in the appropriate personnel and technology can be quite expensive. Therefore, a lot of the hedge funds outsource this task to independent fund administrators. Following is the overall ranking of the hedge fund administrators as per Institutional Investor's Alpha Magazine 2007 Awards:

Ranking	Administrator
1	Goldman, Sachs & Co.
2	Admiral Administration
3	Morgan Stanley

A custodian is a third party that physically holds the assets of a hedge fund, but usually the fund's administrator will also serve as the fund's custodian. All the stocks, bonds, cash, and other physical security certificates are held by the independent custodian. This is supposed to provide an extra layer of comfort for the fund investor.

There are several benefits of an independent fund administrator and custodian. This provides the investor with assurance that the fund's assets are being held by an independent third party, and the valuation is also being done independently. The fund administrator receives trade confirmations directly from the executing broker and is able to reconcile the fund's assets to the trades executed and the fund's cash position. The fund administrator also receives the position valuations on a daily basis from the executing brokers and sometimes even performs his own independent valuations. The fund administrator will then use a combination of his own independent valuation and the executing broker's valuations for producing the final NAV numbers. Often, the hedge fund manager will also relinquish signage rights, so the fund administrator has the sole rights to transfer the fund's cash. Based on directions from the fund manager, the administrator will send or receive money from the brokers for margins, send money to the manager for fee payments, and pay other third-party fees related to fund expenses. This is a comforting thought for the investor, as he or she knows that an unscrupulous fund manager cannot transfer the fund's cash to unauthorized accounts. Quite a few of the hedge fund scandals could have been avoided if the hedge fund had a reputable independent administrator. KL Financial and Bernie Madoff, the two scandals we discussed in Chapter 1, did not employ independent fund administrators and were handling their own fund's administration and providing fictitious fund valuations and investor statements. Hedge fund scandal history is littered with several more such examples of misstating fund valuations and transferring funds to unauthorized accounts. Table 5.1 provides a short list stressing the repeating patterns that are very avoidable by performing appropriate operational due diligence on the hedge funds.

The abovementioned services are what an ideal administrator is supposed to provide, but that is not always the case. Some administrators may only provide a subset of these services, while some might have entered into an agreement with the hedge fund manager to alter the nature of those services. Therefore, just the fact that a hedge fund manager has a well-recognized administrator does not always translate to complete and independent administration of the funds. Some of the questions that an investor should ask an administrator are as follows:

1. **Portfolio Valuation:** Is the portfolio valuation really independent or does the hedge fund manager have a say over the valuation of a certain number of securities? As an example, when I was running my hedge fund, Predator Capital, my administrator was GlobeOp Financial

TABLE 5.1 Hedge Fund Scandal History

Fund Manager	Date	Loss	Description
Nicholas Cosmo	January 2009	> $370 million	Fictitious account statements. Improper channeling of funds.
Joseph S. Forte	January 2009	> $50 million	Fictitious account statements.
Arthur Nadel	January 2009	> $300 million	Fictitious account statements.
Bayou Management	September 2005	> $450 million	Gross overstatement of NAV and disseminating fictitious statements.
Philadelphia Alternative Asset Management	July 2005	$140 million	Hid losses from investors.
Portus Alternative Asset Management	February 2005	$18 million	Improper channeling of funds.

Services. In our agreement, we had stated that the management company would be able to provide pricing sources for certain hard-to-value emerging market securities. In this case, the portfolio valuation would end up being different from the one provided by the prime brokers, but would not be evident to the investor unless he or she looked at the Offering Memorandum's Fund Valuation section very closely. There are some hedge funds that value the entire portfolio themselves, without any independent oversight of the administrator at all.

2. **Right to Move Funds:** Most hedge fund managers will sign away the authority to transfer funds to the administrator, but not all. There is no reason, in my opinion, why a hedge fund manager cannot relinquish fund transfer rights to the administrator. After all, it just takes a phone call or an email to the administrator asking him to transfer funds to a client or a prime broker, but it provides a huge sigh of relief to the investor that his or her funds are not being illegally transferred to an unauthorized account.

3. **Straight Through Processing (STP):** Most fund administration agreements will entail that the fund administrator receives trade confirmations directly from the prime brokers. This limits the scope for rogue traders to hide trades. Many storied Wall Street trading desks and even entire banks have been decimated by rogue traders who have hidden trade tickets in their drawers and taken advantage of loopholes in the system. Kidder Peabody, a white-shoe investment-banking firm founded in 1865, was led to its demise in 1994 because of such an instance. STP will ensure that all confirmations and details of all trades executed by the hedge fund are being submitted to the fund's administrator directly by the brokers, without first going through the hedge fund manager's office.

An independent administrator and custodian should prevent most outright fraud and Ponzi schemes, although there are ways that an unscrupulous hedge fund manager can get around these as well. One such example of a well-orchestrated fraud was conducted by Lancer Capital Management, according to the *SEC versus Michael Lauer and Lancer Management Group LLC* case submitted to the United States Southern District Court of Florida in July 2003. Lancer Capital was investing in small and mid cap companies that had very small traded volumes. Lancer described its trading strategy as investing in "fallen angels," that is, companies that were not actively covered by Wall Street analysts but with perceived value according to Lancer's research. One of the companies that Lancer was invested in was Fidelity First Financial Corporation (Fidelity First). Lancer held stock in Fidelity First valued at close to $240 million while Fidelity

First's total assets were a mere $25,000 as of December 31, 2002. Where did this valuation of $240 million come from? Simple: Lancer manipulated the stock price to generate those valuations. According to SEC's allegations, "Defendants' manipulative trading practices consisted of purchasing blocks of certain thinly traded stocks, generally at increasing prices, at or near the close of the last trading days of the month (commonly known in the securities industry as 'Marking the Close'). Defendants made these purchases through brokerage accounts they controlled and with the funds' assets. These purchases were made with the intent to raise the closing market price of certain stocks in the funds' portfolios. The ultimate objective of the scheme was to overinflate the funds' performances and NAVs to attract additional prospective investors and/or induce investors to invest additional funds, and thereby result in increased management and performance fees. On December 31, 2002, at the end of the last trading day of the year, Lancer Management placed two orders for Fidelity First stock which comprised 100 percent of retail purchases on that date." In a situation like this, the fund's administrator would receive the stock's closing price from market sources and provide an independent fund valuation. While the fund managers would not be directly involved in pricing their portfolio, they clearly would have violated securities laws and indirectly marked their portfolio at fictitious levels.

Market manipulation to generate spurious returns, as in the case of Lancer Capital, is not the only pitfall that an independent administrator cannot spot and therefore stop. The hedge fund manager can drift from his stated trading strategy, get too concentrated in a particular market sector, or take on too much risk. It is not an administrator's responsibility to monitor those constraints. While some administrators will provide risk-reporting services as well, these are mostly limited to producing a measure of various risk parameters in the portfolio. The investor needs somebody who can understand the composition of the portfolio, the source of returns in a portfolio, as well as understand and make sure that the risk parameters are within stated and reasonable constraints. That ongoing due diligence cannot be provided by the fund's administrator and is the investor's responsibility and should be delegated to the experts in trading and risk management fields.

Auditors/Accountants

Hedge funds hire independent auditors and accountants to perform two key functions, auditing and tax services. A hedge fund's legal structure usually involves four or more individual companies. Some of these companies will be based domestically in the United States and some will be based offshore, in a tax haven like the Cayman Islands. The auditor will perform a year-end audit of the company's financial statements and capital accounts in accordance with GAAP (Generally Accepted Accounting Principles). The auditor will independently verify the fund's NAV (Net Asset Value) as well as the AUM (Assets Under Management).

Hedge funds also have complex tax issues. The accountants will advise the hedge funds on responsive and creative tax planning with respect to securities transactions to ensure optimum tax benefit. They will also prepare K1 (partnership tax filing) statements for the U.S.–domiciled investors in the fund as well as the tax returns for the U.S.–domiciled companies of the hedge fund.

The presence of an independent and reputable auditor is a very important part of the due diligence process of a hedge fund. A look at the recent hedge fund frauds shows that Bayou Capital, where investors lost $450 million, had set up a phony audit firm. Bernie Madoff, where investors lost $65 billion, had a three-person audit firm that was most likely in cahoots with Madoff. KL Financial plainly refused to get its returns audited, and it was the insistence of its investors for an audit that brought the scam to light. Given the complexity of the hedge fund strategies and the esoteric nature of some of the positions that the fund might be holding, it is essential that the auditor have the requisite skill set to be able to perform an appropriate audit. Just as an independent fund administrator will reduce the chance of a fraud, an independent and reliable auditor will also act as a safeguard. But neither of these two service providers can eliminate the need for ongoing strategy and risk due diligence that can only be performed by experts in the trading and risk management fields.

Following is the ranking of the hedge fund auditors as per Institutional Investor's Alpha Magazine 2007 Awards:

Ranking	Auditor/Accountant
1	BDO Seidman
2	Rothstein Kass & Co.
3	Deloitte Touche Tohmatsu

There are several very important points for an investor to consider when looking at the audited financial statements of a hedge fund:

1. **Garbage In–Garbage Out:** This term is very popular in the world of computer software; i.e., a computer's algorithms will spit out an answer assuming the integrity of the variables fed into it. The same applies to a hedge fund auditor. An auditor relies on records and documents supplied from the fund's administrator and the prime brokers. The auditor then reconciles these records to the financial statements of the fund. If

the records and documents supplied to the auditor are doctored, i.e., garbage, then the audit will be performed on those garbage numbers and garbage audit will come out as well. This is exactly what happened in the case of the Bernie Madoff scandal. Maxam Capital Management, a fund of funds, invested its entire $280 million with Bernie Madoff, then sued its own auditor, McGladrey & Pullen LLP and Goldstein Golub Kessler LLP for negligence. Maxam's auditors relied on the documents supplied by Madoff Investment Securities to ensure that Maxam's financial statements were accurate, but Maxam Capital claims that its auditors should have verified the veracity of Madoff's documents as well. I am not qualified to comment on this dispute, and this case resides with the Connecticut state courts. I think it is a desperate attempt by Maxam Capital to try to lay off blame for its complete failure of fiduciary responsibilities, but nonetheless, this should highlight the importance of Garbage In–Garbage Out aspect of an audit.

2. **Annual Versus Monthly Returns:** Most hedge fund audits are done on an annual basis (cost being the major decisive factor), therefore the auditors tend to reconcile the fund's year-end accounts and provide an annual return for the fund. The auditors would have to do considerably more work to audit the monthly returns of the fund. Therefore, the fund's audit report may or may not be verifying the monthly returns, but just the annual returns. Therefore, if a hedge fund states that its returns are audited, the question to follow should be whether just the annual results are audited or the monthly returns as well.

Prime Brokers

A prime broker is the conduit between the hedge fund manager and the markets; therefore, by definition a prime broker is a major Wall Street brokerage house. A prime broker will provide a package of services to the hedge fund manager to enable him to access the markets and execute his strategy, as well as provide clearing and settlement services for the securities. Long-short managers who have to borrow stocks or bonds to short rely on their prime broker's network to source those securities. Hedge funds often deploy leverage and therefore need to borrow cash. Prime brokers are the source of that funding requirement. Once a trade is executed, the trade needs to be settled, and the cash needs to be sent to or received from the counterparty. The prime broker provides these clearing services as well. Oftentimes, the prime broker will serve as the custodian of the securities, unless the manager has designated a separate custodian, in which case the securities are transferred to the custodian. The relationship between the hedge fund manager and his prime broker(s) is a very crucial one. A year like 2008 saw a lot of havoc being created for the hedge fund managers as a result of an upheaval among the Wall Street banks. Lehman Brothers and Bear Stearns were prime brokers for several major hedge funds. The bankruptcy of Lehman Brothers has resulted in locking up or an outright loss of a lot of hedge fund assets. The credit crisis and the risk averseness that has followed have resulted in the cutting of lending lines and thereby the crucial leverage required by the hedge fund managers. This has resulted in forced liquidation of positions as a result of de-leveraging of portfolios and wild swings in securities prices and losses for the industry. This is not the first time the financial industry has suffered forced de-leveraging with the previous bout in 1990–1991 and again in 1998 during the Asian crisis. For the next several years, the hedge funds will be running a lot less levered, but once the risk averseness subsides, as it always does, you can be rest assured that leverage will be back in full force.

Prime Broker as a Capital Introducer Prime brokers also provide a very crucial service to the hedge fund industry, and that of a matchmaker. While they do not usually raise capital for the hedge funds, they will provide capital introduction services by matching up the hedge fund manager with qualified hedge fund investors. Due to their investment banking and asset management franchises, the prime brokers have contacts with pools of capital around the world that invests in alternative strategies. This is very attractive for a startup hedge fund manager as he is able to get access to several investors in one place instead of traveling all over the world to pitch his strategy. An important thing for an investor to understand is that a capital-introducing prime broker, even with a name like Goldman Sachs or Morgan Stanley, is just an introducer and is not in any way vetting the manager or his strategy. The prime broker is not getting paid, directly, by the manager or the investors for this matchmaking service, and it is the investor's responsibility to conduct his or her complete due diligence on the manager and his strategy.

Following is the ranking of the hedge fund prime brokers as per Institutional Investor's Alpha Magazine 2007 Awards:

Ranking	Prime Broker
1	Morgan Stanley
2	Goldman, Sachs & Co.
3	Banc of America Securities

Third-Party Marketers

As the hedge fund industry has grown, so has the outsourcing of capital raising for the hedge funds. While most large hedge funds have their own internal marketing departments that are housed with seasoned sales professionals from Wall Street banks, the vast majority of the hedge funds outsource the capital raising efforts to third-party marketers. The third-party marketers will employ seasoned investment marketing experts who have a Rolodex of clients that will include pension funds, high net worth individuals, endowments, and funds of hedge funds. The third-party marketer will help the hedge fund manager in designing the pitch book as well as the marketing pitch and setup meetings with the potential investors. The hedge fund manager will then explain his strategy to the investor who will make the investment decision. It is in the marketer's economic interest that the meeting results in an investment as he is compensated with a certain percentage of the fees that the hedge fund manager collects. The marketer will typically receive 20 percent of the annual management fees as well as 20 percent of the performance fees on the capital he introduces to the hedge fund manager, as long as that capital stays invested with the manager.

This role is similar to what the prime broker's capital introduction team does for the hedge fund manager as well, except that the prime broker does not get paid by the hedge fund manager directly for any capital raised. Just because the third-party marketer is getting paid a fee, it does not imply that he is necessarily qualified to vet the manager's strategy or that he is performing necessary due diligence for the investor. In fact, a look at the backgrounds of most third-party marketers shows experience with marketing and client relationships and rarely any experience trading capital on a Wall Street trading desk. When I was starting my hedge fund in 2003, I distinctly remember a meeting with a third-party marketer who was regarded as one of the best in the industry. As I did not have an office space at that point, we decided to meet in the lobby of the Hilton Hotel in midtown Manhattan, a place quite popular for hedge fund meetings. I explained my strategy, which was a global macro strategy focused on the Asian markets. I also told him that I concentrated in currencies and interest rate derivatives. After I spoke for about 45 minutes, while he nodded his head, I asked him if he had any questions about my strategy. His first comment was that he did not think there were enough trading opportunities in Asia. After living in Asia and trading the markets for over six years I certainly thought that there were plenty of opportunities even back in 2003, but this marketer who had never been to Asia, never traded a single day in his life, or even bothered to research those markets had firmly drawn his conclusions. I had also told him that I did not trade stocks and did all my interest rate trading through the derivatives market, but that did not stop him from asking me how I would borrow securities in Asia and what my stock shorting mechanism was. Interest rate derivatives are off balance sheet instruments and do not require borrowing of securities, but by this point I was so disgusted with this so-called expert that I ended the meeting and headed to the bar in shock and dismay. That was 2003, but even six years later nothing has changed regarding the level of expertise of a third-party marketer. They are good at client relationships and marketing a manager for which they get paid by the hedge fund manager. An investor should not assume that the marketer is introducing him or her to the appropriate strategy or a good manager; the burden of due diligence rests squarely on the investor's shoulders. The victims of Bernie Madoff placed their trust in the unofficial third-party marketers, like Robert Jaffe of Palm Beach, without understanding that the burden of due diligence lay on them.

Regulators

There has been a lot of debate about hedge fund regulation in the United States, and much has been misunderstood about the level of protection provided to the investors by the SEC and the like. A typical public investment company domiciled in the United States is required to be registered with the U.S. Securities and Exchange Commission (SEC). A common example of such an investment company is a mutual fund. Such a company has reporting requirements and is also subject to strict limitations on short-selling, use of leverage, and prohibition from charging incentive or performance fees.

Although hedge funds fall within the statutory definition of an investment company, the limited-access and private nature of hedge funds permits them to operate outside the SEC's purview. The two major exemptions are set forth in Sections 3(c)1 and 3(c)7 of the Investment Company Act of 1940. Those exemptions are for funds with hundred or fewer investors (a "3(c) 1 Fund") and funds where the investors are "qualified purchasers" (a "3(c) 7 Fund"). A qualified purchaser is an individual with over $5 million in investment assets. To comply with these regulations, hedge funds cannot be offered or advertised to the general public and are sold via private placement under the Securities Act of 1933.

For the hedge funds, the tradeoff of operating under these exemptions is that they have fewer investors to sell to, but they have few government-imposed restrictions on their investment strategies as well. Clearly, the benefits for the hedge fund manager in not registering with the SEC are many, especially for the smaller hedge funds, as they do not have to deal with the cumbersome and expensive processes of a government bureaucracy. But there are also benefits in registering with the SEC—the biggest is marketability. When an investor sees that a hedge fund manager is a registered investment advisor with the SEC, it gives him or her a certain sense of comfort that someone is watching over his or her investment. This is a false panacea and akin to hiding your head in the sand like an ostrich. If there is one lesson I want a hedge fund investor to take away from this book, it is that the regulators like the SEC have very little oversight over hedge funds and even less competence to provide the investor with any sense of security. This is especially true for the high net worth individual who has decided to go down the road of hedge fund investing solo, instead of relying on industry experts to do the due diligence.

The Toothless SEC

As the myriad of frauds unfold before our eyes, too often we hear the comments from the duped investors, "Where were the regulators?" In the case of the Madoff Ponzi scheme, Harry Markopolos, who worked for a Madoff rival firm, even submitted a twenty-one-page report to the SEC's New York office in the fall of 2005 citing a series of 29 red flags why he believed that the Madoff operation was a giant Ponzi scheme. In fact, he approached Edward Manion at the SEC's Boston office as early as 2000 with his doubts about Madoff's operation. Armed with all the red flags and after a period of almost eight years of due diligence, the SEC kept giving Madoff a clean bill of health. Madoff would have kept running his Ponzi scheme if he had not run into the credit crisis of 2008. In fact, the regulators never caught him; the market crisis and the subsequent redemptions from his investors forced him to confess on December 11, 2008. Regulators have not only failed in protecting the investor from hedge fund frauds but also from the frauds committed by publicly traded corporations like Enron, WorldCom, HealthSouth, and others. The list is long and will continue to get longer, because the regulators are not staffed with the appropriate personnel who possess the necessary skill and experience to conduct the required due diligence.

After the recent spate of frauds and scandals in the hedge fund industry, the politicians will be clamoring for more regulation. They will most likely require hedge funds to register with the SEC and impose rules of transparency and reporting. The important thing for the regulators to understand is that they need to impose the right regulation and not regulation for the sake of it. Regulation should mandate the use of qualified and independent audit firms and administrators. As shown earlier, quite a few of the frauds and scandals could have been exposed if the hedge funds had been required to provide independent fund valuations. Another benefit of regulation would be to have the hedge funds provide detailed risk reports to their investors. The regulators could stipulate the risk parameters on a standardized basis that the hedge fund manager has to submit to his investors on a monthly basis. Then it will be up to the investor to hire the proper trading and risk management professionals to decipher these reports and provide suitable advice to the investors. The SEC should not get into the business of policing the amount of risk carried by hedge funds. Hedge funds are investment vehicles designed to meet the risk and return demands of sophisticated investors, therefore it is not the SEC's job to monitor the risk taken by hedge funds, but the investor's. While transparency is crucial for free markets to function properly, so is the principle of market discipline. And that is the key difference between capitalism and statism.

Any curbs on the investment style regarding the use of leverage, derivatives or short selling, or curbs on incentive fees will only result in the hedge fund managers relocating to an offshore location. Any mandates on increasing transparency at a position or trade level will be useless as well. Unlike a mutual fund manager, hedge fund managers are traders, and they often change their positions multiple times a month, if not every day. Therefore, by the time any position disclosure is made, it would be very stale. Additionally, most hedge fund managers would not like to have their portfolio put on display, given that it is their proprietary technology for which they charge a handsome fee.

The SEC is staffed with lawyers who see their job as solely enforcing the legal stipulations governing the financial industry. They do not have the staffers with experience in the financial industry, such as traders, trading managers, and risk management personnel, who can detect the frauds before they happen. As Harry Markopolos said in a recent Congressional testimony, "the SEC needs personnel who can take apart and put back together the trading strategies that are employed at the hedge funds to be able to detect fraudulent activities." Only then would they have the capability to detect frauds like Bayou Capital, KL Financial, and Bernie Madoff before they happen and actually protect the investing community. But even after the recent spate of scandals, this lesson seems to be lost on the SEC. The current chairman, Mary Schapiro, is a lawyer by training and a bureaucrat by experience as was the director of enforcement, Linda Thomsen. Linda Thomsen recently resigned and has been replaced by Robert Khuzami, a former federal prosecutor and last, a managing director and general counsel of investment firm Deutsche Bank. David Ignatius of the *Washington Post* recently commented on President Obama's picks for his administration by stating in the March 28, 2009 edition of the *Economist*, "the administration is as thin on business experience as a Hyde Park book club." The same can be said about the SEC. The SEC's insistence on staffing the senior ranks with lawyers instead of financial industry practitioners will make it very hard to instill confidence in the minds of investors who have been severely burnt by the recent spate of investment scandals.

CONCLUSION

In this chapter, I have covered the typical service providers hired by a hedge fund manager to provide the needed legal, accounting, marketing, administrative and regulatory guidance to run a hedge fund. Most hedge fund investors will give a cursory glance at the Offering Memorandum of a hedge fund or the administrator, prime brokerage, and accounting agreements that exist between these service providers and the hedge fund. The investors cannot be blamed for this, as these agreements are verbose and inundated with legal terms that are very hard to decipher. Just because a hedge fund manager has an external auditor, does not automatically mean that the audited returns of that hedge fund can be taken as gospel. The Madoff Ponzi scheme proved that. Likewise, just because the hedge fund is using a reputable administrator does not imply that the fund's NAV (net asset value) is accurate. The devil is in the detail. And the investors need expert advice to decipher these details. Therefore, I would highly advise both the high net worth Individuals as well as the Institutional investors to avail themselves of true experts before foraying into the hedge fund investing space.

The second major point I want to highlight in this chapter is that the regulatory bodies should see their role in the hedge fund industry as no more than mandating increased transparency. And the investors should not rely on the regulators to perform the requisite due diligence for them. It is entirely the investor's responsibility, to take the information provided by the hedge funds and determine if the investment is prudent or not. Risk and returns go hand in hand and if we truly cherish the ideals of a free market economy, then the investors have to take responsibility for their own investment decisions. At the end of the day, the investors are the best regulators, as they control the flow of capital and they should demand the requisite information in return for the fees they pay to the hedge fund industry.

CHAPTER 6

Funds of Hedge Funds

In my previous chapters, I have tried to outline the expertise and the training required to become a hedge fund manager and the complex nature of the hedge fund strategies. I have also shown the level of due diligence required, not just at the onset of the investment but also on an ongoing basis, to ensure the safety of your investment in a hedge fund. Furthermore, I have tried to illustrate the type of due diligence to be expected from auditors and regulators and how at the end of the day it is the investors' responsibility to engage the proper trading and risk management professionals to stay on top of their hedge fund investments. While a few investors do invest in hedge funds directly through their own due diligence, a vast majority of them outsource the due diligence and investment decisions to hedge fund professionals like the funds of hedge funds. According to the *Alpha* magazine, nearly 40 percent of all hedge fund assets are with the fund of hedge funds, which have been trusted with the task of investing in hedge funds. The fund of funds industry has failed at this fiduciary responsibility. In this chapter, I plan to illustrate the philosophy and mechanism used by the funds of funds in making their investment decisions and how it is flawed and needs to be radically altered.

PHILOSOPHY AND SERVICES

To understand the philosophy and the services offered by a fund of hedge funds, I went to the website of two of the oldest and the largest funds of hedge funds, Fairfield Greenwich Group (FGG) and Tremont Capital. Until recently these two institutions were one of the most respected, but after the Madoff scandal, they are also the most reviled funds of funds. I deliberately picked these two institutions to illustrate the problems with the model of hedge fund investing. You will notice that the philosophies of both the institutions are quite sound; therefore, logic dictates that the flaw in their model must lie in the execution of these philosophies. FGG's investment philosophy requires that the hedge fund managers it invests in abide by the following principles (source: www.fggus.com):

■ **Full Transparency:** Transparency provides the ability to analyze and ensure that portfolio managers are complying with strategy-specific investment limitations, and to better understand and monitor changes in their investment behavior in changing markets.

■ **Liquid Portfolios:** Liquid portfolios are important to protecting the portfolio in volatile markets, permitting redemption liquidity with less disruption, and also removing or greatly reducing many of the illiquid portfolio pricing issues that create significant risks in a number of other hedge funds.

■ **Low Correlation:** FGG funds seek genuine low correlation to the broader markets and to genuinely capture Alpha.

■ **Low Relative Leverage:** Leverage may increase returns, but it also increases risk and volatility, and reduces a portfolio manager's margin of error. If they use leverage at all, FGG's core funds generally use leverage toward the lower end of the risk continuum for their strategy, and managing leverage risk is a key concern of our ongoing risk monitoring.

■ **Low Volatility:** The pursuit of lower volatility has led FGG funds to have a strong history of delivering smoother, more moderate returns over time, rather than the higher volatility—and higher potential for "surprises"—that typically accompanies a "high returns" investment strategy.

Tremont's "Value-Added Proposition" claims the following (source: www.tremont.com):

■ **Strategy-Focused Investment Process:** Tremont's investment teams are organized by strategy. This enables us to integrate top down and bottom up decision-making to enhance risk-adjusted returns and provide customized solutions for Tremont client needs.

■ **An Experienced Investment Team:** Tremont has a veteran investment team with strong and diverse professional backgrounds.

■ **Risk Management:** Risk assessment is integrated into every aspect of our investment process.

■ **Global Reach:** Tremont's long-standing global presence, through offices in the United States, Asia, and Europe has provided access to local opportunities and insights globally.

■ **Strong Infrastructure and Corporate Oversight:** Experienced senior management staff with over 100 years of collective experience oversee the financial, operational, legal, and compliance structure of the firm.

To summarize a fund of fund's investment philosophy, it invests in diversified strategies and managers with varying styles to capture alpha (excess returns) that are uncorrelated to the equity markets. It further wants managers to produce this alpha with very low volatility and by utilizing very little leverage. And finally, it wants to be able to redeem its investments at short notice and have the manager provide complete transparency so it can ensure the manager is adhering to his stated strategy and risk parameters. To implement this philosophy, the fund of funds touts experienced investment and risk management personnel backed by a strong infrastructure and a global outlook.

FAILURE OF FIDUCIARY DUTIES

The above-stated investing philosophies of fund of funds are very sound, and if they were backed by the proper personnel and infrastructure, the industry would be running without too many hiccups. Alas! That is not the case. Both Tremont and FGG completely failed in executing their own philosophies and were duped by Bernie Madoff's Ponzi scheme. Tremont lost $3 billion, more than half of its assets under management and is being sued by its clients, while FGG lost $7.5 billion or half its assets as well. These two funds of funds are not the only ones to be duped by Madoff. Following is a list of funds of funds that were all well established and touted the appropriate due diligence measures, but were also invested with Madoff (source: *Wall Street Journal*):

- **Fairfield Greenwich Group.** The alternative investment specialist said in a statement on its website it had invested approximately $7.5 billion in vehicles connected to Madoff, or half of its assets.
- **Tremont Holdings.** The hedge fund group's Rye Investment Management unit had virtually all of its assets invested with Madoff and lost roughly $3 billion.
- **Ascot Partners.** According to a *Wall Street Journal* report, the fund, where former GMAC chairman Jacob Ezra Merkin is a money manager, has an exposure of $1.8 billion.
- **Access International Advisors.** According to a report by Bloomberg, Access has an exposure of $1.4 billion.
- **Reichmuth & Co.** Reichmuth & Co. said in a statement the exposure of fund Reichmuth Mattehorn amounted to about $325 million.

- **Man Group.** The U.K. hedge fund said RMF, its fund of funds business, has about $360 million invested in two funds that are directly or indirectly sub-advised by Madoff.
- **Maxam Capital Management.** The fund has lost about $280 million on funds invested with Madoff, a source familiar with the situation said.
- **EIM Group.** Bill Glass, partner and head of business development at the EIM Group, said the group has under $230 million of exposure to Madoff.
- **Credit Industriel ET Commercial.** Credit Mutuel's unit CIC said it could have a maximum of 90 million euros exposure to Madoff.
- **Austin Capital Management.** The company managed money for the Massachusetts state pension fund, which lost $12 million with Madoff, it said.
- **Kingate Global Fund.** The $2.8 billion hedge fund run by FIM lost all its assets to Madoff Investment Securities.
- **Bramdean Alternatives.** U.K. asset manager, headed by well-known fund manager Nicola Horlick, said 9.5 percent of its holdings were exposed to Madoff.
- **Union Bancaire Privee.** The world's largest fund of hedge funds has lost about 1 billion francs, according to Le Temps, citing unnamed banking sources.

Besides the recent Madoff scandal, which exposed the flaws with the funds of funds industry, the hedge fund investors have been complaining for years that the fees charged by the funds of funds do not justify the services they provide. The hedge fund managers are no fans of the funds of funds either. The hedge fund managers complain that the funds of funds are performance chasers and do not understand the strategies they invest in. Therefore, their investment decisions are driven not by rational measures but by greed and fear. Let us explore how a fund of funds goes about executing its investment philosophy before we get into the problems and the solutions.

STATISTICAL BUCKETING BY STRATEGY

A typical fund of hedge funds will invest in a portfolio of 10 to 100 underlying hedge fund managers. The fund of funds usually has a bucket allocation system based on hedge fund strategies. Therefore, the buckets would constitute long-short equity strategies, global macro strategies, relative value strategies, etc. It will predefine these buckets as well as the percentage of its assets to be allocated to these buckets based on its market research. It might also do a further subdivision of its buckets based on geography. If it feels that the opportunities in the Asian markets would exceed the opportunities in the European markets, it might allocate a larger percentage of its assets to the Asian sub-bucket.

The next task is actually picking hedge fund managers to put in these buckets. The approach to investing in hedge funds was and still is a backward-looking data mining approach. A typical fund of funds will have a massive database of hedge fund managers that it monitors. It will track the asset size, performance history, and the strategy bucket of the hedge fund manager. It will receive some of this information through third-party database services and some directly from the manager. Hedge fund managers generally send out monthly newsletters in which they state their performance numbers, some market color and information about their portfolio. The fund of funds will then run one of the readily available statistics packages like SAS or MATLAB on this data to pick managers whose returns are not correlated to its existing portfolio. This will result in lowering the fund of fund's portfolio volatility and thereby allow it to take on more risk. Most funds of funds utilize leverage to enhance their risk and thereby the returns. As most funds of funds use the same statistics packages and the same portfolio construction principles, learned at the top business schools in the country, they all seem to come up with a similar group of hedge funds to invest in. It really makes one wonder about the added-value component of a fund of funds. Is it running a commercially available statistics package on backward-looking historical performance numbers? Well, that certainly cannot be worth the extra layer of 1 to 2 percent annual management fees and 10 to 15 percent performance fees charged by the funds of funds. I approached a fund of funds manager with the above stated argument, and he proceeded to lecture me on the other value-added services that a fund of funds provides, such as due diligence on the manager, ongoing oversight, access to closed managers, and consolidated reporting. As a hedge fund manager myself, I have had close to 200 meetings with funds of funds and have experienced their due diligence process and ongoing oversight that I would like to share with the readers.

DUE DILIGENCE AND THE ANALYST

After a fund of funds' statistics package identifies a hedge fund manager, the fund of funds contacts the manager for a due diligence meeting. A hedge fund manager can pretty much predict when he will be flooded with calls from fund of funds. Most funds of funds have set a randomly assigned target of monitoring the last three to six months of a hedge fund's performance. Therefore, a new manager tries very hard to produce steady positive numbers for two consecutive quarters to attract the fund of funds, and a manager who has had a down period also needs three to six months of steady positive performance to get back in the good graces of the fund of funds. The initial due diligence meeting is generally held with analysts. These analysts are usually freshly minted MBAs with little or no experience in the financial industry. They are smart and have attended the top business schools in the country, so they know what a stock is and that the price of a bond goes down when interest rates go up (a favorite interview question for finance MBAs). They have read about hedge funds in newspapers and financial journals, especially the year-end issues that talk about the nine- or ten-figure paychecks. They have dreamed of becoming a hedge fund manager themselves, but due to the Darwinian nature of the financial industry have instead found themselves working at a fund that allocates capital to a hedge fund. They walk into the due diligence meeting wide-eyed, awestruck and probably trying to impress the hedge fund manager, rather than the other way around, so they can create an employment opportunity for themselves down the road. An analyst makes up for the lack of experience by bringing with him a stack of papers with preprinted questions. Hedge fund industry organizations like the Alternative Investment Management Association Ltd. (AIMA) have even taken the trouble to produce these questionnaires for the hedge fund investor. Therefore, a hedge fund manager can expect to receive a barrage of exactly the same questions and in the same order from every fund of funds, advisor, or consultant. I had reached a point in my meetings with funds of funds that I would start speaking and giving them the answers in the order in which I knew the questions would be asked.

Before the due diligence meeting even starts, the manager needs to have a strategy that can fit into one of the predefined buckets. The fund of funds operates on a system of predefined allocation buckets, i.e., long-short equity, global macro, etc. God forbid, if the hedge fund manager actually comes up with a new idea or a strategy that overlaps two or three of these predefined buckets. How do inexperienced young graduates deal with this problem? Well, some of them will put the manager in a holding pile, which basically means that "we love your strategy, it is a proven alpha generator, but down the road when we have created a bucket for you to fit in, we will give you a call." I remember having a very good meeting with a fund of funds: He liked my low volatility, Asia-focused macro strategy executed solely with derivatives instruments. The big question was that he did not know whether to put me in his global macro bucket, emerging markets bucket, or low volatility bucket. After pondering for a long time, he told me that to receive an allocation, I would have to change my strategy so I could fit into one of his predefined allocation buckets. I shook my head in disbelief and walked out of the meeting cursing the absurdity of the process. The reader should not be too surprised by the fund of fund's dilemma and subsequent solution. The best analogy I can draw is by comparing this experience to a visit to a doctor's office. Say the doctor was not a qualified practitioner but someone who had been given a book with a list of common ailments and their prescribed cures. How would that doctor deal with a patient who walks in with kidney stones? Either the patient would be told to come back when the good doctor's book had a section on kidney stones or told to come back when he had transformed his disease into a common cold. Clearly, neither the patients, nor the physician community, nor the regulatory community would ever let such a physician practice medicine. But obviously the standards are different when handling an investor's money rather than his health, although the effects of mishandling both are quite dire and often deadly. Thierry Magon de La Villehuchet, 65, who co-founded Access International, an investor in Bernie Madoff, committed suicide in late December 2008 after the alleged Ponzi scheme came to light.

WHAT'S IN A NAME?

Once the hedge fund manager has made sure that he has the strategy that would fit into one of the predefined buckets, he has to make sure that his fund has an appropriate name as well. Has one noticed the names of hedge funds? While some are named after their founders, like SAC Capital after its founder Steve A. Cohen or Soros after its founder George Soros, and some reflect their strategy, like Renaissance Technologies, most others are given ultraconservative names. There are several examples of funds with words like Safe Harbor, Long View, and Evergreen in their names. While such fund names are meant to inspire feelings of confidence and stability, there is very little correlation between performance and the fund's nomenclature. Some funds are named to inspire a sense of blue-bloodedness like Fairfield Greenwich, which might have helped its owners in raising capital from the blue-blooded gentry around the world but did not prevent the fund from bleeding red due to shoddy management. Hedge fund names like Maverick, Pirate, or Predator are very few and far between. These names show some degree of original thinking and entrepreneurialism, the base ingredients of alpha generation.

I named my fund Predator Capital, and our motto was "For when the markets foster a herd mentality." I thought the hedge fund industry was the epitome of Darwin's theory of "the survival of the fittest" and the name of one's hedge fund should embody that spirit. After all, the hedge fund industry was founded to break the bureaucratic shackles of the banking world and give the enterprising mind an opportunity to come up with creative ways of generating returns. I thought that this sense of enthusiasm and creativity should be reflected unabashedly in the name of the fund as well. I had mixed success with the name. Some investors loved the name, some mocked it before even bothering to discuss the strategy, while one European investor even asked me, "Does the name Predator mean that you prey on your investors?" It is a real shame that the largest service industry in the world, in terms of capital, still lets perception and salesmanship trump the basics of financial innovation. Bernie Madoff clearly understood this mindset very well and abused it for over fifteen years to his advantage.

THE AIMA DUE DILIGENCE QUESTIONNAIRE

Once the preliminary details like strategy and name of the fund have been appropriately boxed, the fund of fund's analyst will diligently step through the AIMA questionnaire. In all fairness, the AIMA questionnaire is very thorough and covers all aspects of a hedge fund's operations and procedures. It has detailed questions broken out under the following sections:

Investment Manager Information
Execution & Trading
Compliance
Legal
Business Continuity
Fund Details
Fees
Fund Administrator
Fund Pricing
Prime Brokers
Custodian
Auditor
Third-Party Marketers
Fund Assets
Capacity Management
Redemption Procedures
Investor Base

Fund Performance

Drawdowns

Investment Strategy

Portfolio Construction

Risk

Leverage

Hedging

Liquidity

Diversification

External Controls

Investor Service/Reporting

Taxation

The above-described AIMA questionnaire has several sub-sections to it, and once it has been duly filled, it can be as long as a hundred pages. One must wonder that if a fund of funds does perform its stated due diligence and asks all the questions in this AIMA questionnaire, the possibility of fraud or nasty surprises should be all but eliminated. I am sure that is what the executives at Fairfield Greenwich and Tremont must have told their investors about their due diligence on Madoff, yet Madoff managed to dupe his investors for over 15 years. The funds of funds that were invested in an Amaranth or a Long Term Capital Management must have also convinced their investors about the level of ongoing due diligence conducted in these funds as well. The usefulness of this AIMA questionnaire in the hands of a novice is about as much as that of a Formula 1 Ferrari in the hands of Homer Simpson. In the next chapter, I will explain how the funds of funds lack the tools for identifying the red flags in a hedge fund manager's answers to an AIMA-type questionnaire.

After a hedge fund manager has satisfied the analyst's AIMA questionnaire, the next and final step is a meeting with the Chief Investment Officer (CIO) of the fund of funds. While the initial meeting is held at the fund of fund's office or as a telephone call, the meeting with the CIO is usually held at the hedge fund manager's office. This is termed as the onsite due diligence meeting. The CIO will generally show up with several more analysts in tow who will sit down in the conference room and basically go over the AIMA questionnaire again. The onsite visit is usually made to ensure that an office for the hedge fund manager exists with working computers and breathing employees.

WHERE ARE THE EXPERIENCED PROFESSIONALS?

A fund of fund's investment decision making is based on churning historical performance data and not active monitoring of the trading strategies, economic conditions, and trader discipline. Therefore, it is no surprise that the investment committees at the funds of funds comprise people who have extensive experience in statistical analysis, traditional asset management, relationship banking, marketing, legal, and other fine professions. The lines between an asset raiser and an asset investor at a fund of funds have been blurred, and often the same person serves both roles. And herein lies the fundamental problem with the fund of funds as well as the hedge fund allocation industry as a whole. The investment committees do not have professionals who have traded capital and managed traders. This is the most crucial skill set required to be able to conduct meaningful due diligence on a hedge fund manager as well as to ensure that he stays within his stated strategy and risk parameters. Imagine that a football franchise wants to recruit new talent. Instead of sending the coaches to scout the talent, the franchise sends stadium builders, groundskeepers, and concession stand employees to do the scouting. As ludicrous as it sounds, that is what the fund of funds investment team and process is akin to.

I was able to access the biographies of some of the funds of funds' investment and risk management professionals to check the teams' experience and here is what I found:

> **Fairfield Greenwich Group** (source: www.fggus.com/guest/brochure .html)
>
> Of the 21 partners listed in the brochure, not one partner had any relevant trading experience to truly understand the trading strategies that they were investing in. It seems that most of the partners had sales experience and that FGG was paying a lot more attention to raising capital than making sure that it had the expertise to deploy it properly. Thus it is no surprise that it never understood Madoff's strategy and his outlandish claims of generating steady returns. FGG lost $7.5 billion, or half of all its assets, to Madoff.
>
> **UBP Asset Management** (source: http://ubpam.com.mt.html)
>
> The following is the excerpt from UBP's website, which states the experience of UBP's CIO: "Roman Igolnikov, the Chief Investment Officer, is responsible for all investment activities of UBPAM and co-leads the Management Committee, which is responsible for governing the day to day matters of the firm. Mr. Igolnikov has 17 years of experience in the financial services industry focusing on strategic asset allocation,

alternative products development, portfolio construction, evaluation and selection of investment managers, and risk management. Prior to joining UBPAM in 2000, Mr. Igolnikov was a Firm Director at Deloitte & Touche LLP where he led the portfolio and securities valuation and risk management practice." Once again we see that UBP, a $50 billion fund of hedge funds has trusted their investment process to someone with no trading experience or who has the capability to understand and evaluate hedge fund strategies. There is little surprise then that UBP lost close to one billion dollars to Madoff.

THE (LACK OF) ONGOING DUE DILIGENCE

Increasing transparency is the new "mantra" in the hedge fund industry. Almost every hedge fund, big or small, provides a newsletter to its investors on a regular basis, usually monthly. This newsletter covers the hedge fund manager's market views, performance of the fund over the past month, the attribution of that performance to the positions in the portfolio, as well as the big positions in the portfolio and the source of major risks. Additionally, hedge funds will conduct regular conference calls with investors and most are very open to entertaining questions from the investors on an ad-hoc basis as well. Quite a few hedge funds will even go as far as to provide daily risk and profit/loss reporting to their investors via email or access to a website. Some third-party vendors also work with a hedge fund's administrator to provide independent risk reporting service. Measurisk, LLC, is one such company that provides risk reporting on Global Equity (Cash and Derivative Products), Interest Rates, Fixed Income, Currency and Commodity sectors. (Source: www.measurisk.com.)

The question is not as much as the lack of transparency and information on hedge fund portfolios as the ability to decipher and understand these risks. As I have shown, the current fund of funds model places more stress on asset raising rather than educated asset deployment. Therefore, all the information on risk and positioning is pretty much meaningless to the fund of funds investor, and those monthly newsletters duly get filed in the do not understand/care for folder. When I ran my hedge fund, we used to send out a monthly newsletter explaining in great detail our portfolio positioning, the views backing those positions, and return attributions. I am sure that the only section of our monthly newsletter the fund of funds cared to read was the section on returns. It was quite amusing that after trading the CNY (Chinese Yuan) for more than a year and mentioning it in every monthly newsletter, a fund of funds asked me what CNY stood for.

The fund of fund's ongoing due diligence process once again comes down to performance history. When a hedge fund manager is producing good steady returns, he will attract all sorts of capital and no in-depth questions on the source of these returns. But when he, like any honest trader, hits a lean patch, he will have capital redemptions from his fund from the trigger-happy and uneducated fund of fund investors. Those very investors will most likely return to the same hedge fund when he starts posting good returns again. In the jargon of a trader, a fund of funds ends up buying high and selling low over and over again.

MULTI-STRATEGY HEDGE FUNDS

Before I finish this chapter on how a fund of funds is set up and operates, I also want to mention the concept of a multi-strategy hedge fund. These hedge funds have recognized the problems and frustrations with the fund of funds industry and have come up with their own solution. A multi-strategy hedge fund looks to emulate a fund of funds by allocating its capital across a diverse set of strategies and asset classes. The multi-strategy fund will employ several portfolio managers within the fund who will be responsible for running the different strategies. There is a centralized risk management and operations infrastructure that supports these different portfolio managers. The multi-strategy hedge fund succeeds in handling the diversification aspect of a fund of funds and most likely also provides the oversight and controls that the fund of funds industry has failed to do. But, what a multi-strategy fund fails at is the lack of diversification in the management, operations, and risk management infrastructure. There is still just one point of failure that can pervade the entire multi-strategy platform. Therefore, a multi-strategy fund will not be able to replace the fund of funds industry. One of the largest and perhaps best run multi-strategy hedge funds is Millennium Partners run by Izzy Englander. Millennium employs 125 different portfolio managers and runs the following investment strategies (source: http://millenniummanagementllc.com/Overview.php):

- Relative Value Fundamental Equity
- Statistical Arbitrage
- Fixed Income Strategies
- Merger Arbitrage
- Closed-End Fund/Asset Arbitrage
- Futures/Currency Arbitrage
- Distressed Investing
- Convertible Arbitrage

- Options Arbitrage
- Other Strategies

A multi-strategy hedge fund is able to eliminate the fund of funds layer of fees; therefore, you will often see institutional investors invest directly into a multi-strategy fund. It would be a real shame to see a fund of funds invest in a multi-strategy fund, as it would be just outsourcing its job and keeping the layer of fees for not doing any work.

Table 6.1 is a list of some of the largest funds of funds, reporting their results to Morningstar database as of October 31, 2007:

TABLE 6.1 Largest Fund of Funds, Ranked by Assets (in millions)

Rank	Fund	Assets
1	Optimal Japan Opp Ireland B JPY	$9,983
2	GAM Multi Japan USD	$9,918
3	Gottex Market Neutral AH	$9,273
4	Permal FX Financials & Futures USD B	$9,011
5	Permal Investment Holdings USD A	$7,508
6	Lyxor/Coast Diversified	$6,700
7	Hermes Japan Fund	$6,057
8	La Fayette Active Value GBP	$5,690
9	Aetos Cap Balanced Onshore	$4,493
10	Gottex Market Neutral Plus JPY	$3,442
11	GMO Multi Strategy	$3,376
12	Morgan Stanley Institutional	$3,175
13	Frank Russell Alt Investment AI	$2,900
14	Arden Alternative Advisers	$2,894
15	Arden Endowment Advisers	$2,754
16	Gems Low Volatility Portfolio EUR	$2,676
17	Optimal Strat US Equity A USD	$2,632
18	Russell Alternative Strategies II	$2,600
19	EnTrust Diversified C	$2,467
20	DB Global Masters USD	$2,418
21	Attalus Multi-Strategy	$2,383
22	EACM Multi-Strategy Composite	$2,300

(Continued)

TABLE 6.1 (*Continued*)

Rank	Fund	Assets
23	Investcorp Balanced	$2,259
24	La Fayette Holdings USD	$2,185
25	Mesirow Equity Opportunity	$2,161
26	Overlook Performance Fund	$2,077
27	Lehman Brothers Alpha Transport	$2,063
28	SAIL Flagship Fund	$2,015
29	JP Morgan Multi-Strategy II	$2,012
30	La Fayette Regular Growth USD	$1,918
31	Ironwood Partners	$1,861
32	Gems Progressive Fund T	$1,837
33	Endowment Master Fund	$1,827
34	Japan Absolute Fund B JPY	$1,789
35	GMO Multi-Strategy Offshore	$1,753
36	Pinnacle Natural Resources	$1,700
37	Mayibentsha Opp Unhedged ZAR	$1,634
38	LCF Leveraged Capital Holdings	$1,626
39	Cadogan Partners	$1,624
40	GMO Multi-Strategy Onshore	$1,623
41	Coast Diversified Fund	$1,610
42	JP Morgan Multi-Strategy	$1,594
43	Optimal Arbitrage A USD	$1,577
44	LCF European Capital Holdings	$1,564
45	The Momentum All Weather	$1,531
46	Eden Rock Structured Finance	$1,530
47	Selectinvest MultiStrategy I USD	$1,520
48	Optimal Multi Strat Ireland A USD	$1,516
49	Momentum All Weather	$1,507

Source: Morningstar Inc., Chicago

CHAPTER 7

An Expert Failure

In the previous chapter on fund of hedge funds we discussed how a fund of funds is set up, its investment philosophy, and the lack of trading and risk management experience among its key staff. The lack of appropriate industry experience among its key investment staff has led the fund of funds to adopt an academic approach to hedge fund investing. A backward-looking data-mining approach tells the fund of funds nothing about the hedge fund's strategy, market views, positioning, or risk in the portfolio. Checking boxes in an AIMA questionnaire will not help the untrained analyst tell the difference between a bookrunner and a proprietary trader or the pitfalls of an onshore versus offshore market arbitrage in emerging markets. In the following sections, I will point out the pitfalls of the existing hedge fund investment and due diligence model that has led to critical mistakes by the funds of hedge funds. Unless the funds of funds radically change their hedge fund investing model, they will continue to fail at delivering the expertise they profess to possess.

USELESSNESS OF HISTORICAL DATA CRUNCHING

Every hedge fund manager's track record comes with a disclaimer, "Past Track Record Is No Indication of Future Performance," yet the funds of funds investors have based their entire investment philosophy around the track record. A fund of funds will claim that the track record of a hedge fund manager will demonstrate his ability to produce steady, uncorrelated returns over bull and bear market cycles as well as his ability to deal with market shocks. The basic precept of relying on past data to predict future outcomes is that the test conditions remain unchanged. Problem with applying a statistical approach to the markets is that the test conditions do not stay constant. No two-market cycles are exactly the same. The 1999 bull market was a result of the run up in Internet stocks while the 2003–2007 period was a result of low interest rates and cheap credit. Similarly, the recent 2008 bear market cannot be compared to any other period in history.

The variables that could affect a trading strategy's returns are also numerous and ever changing because market dynamics are constantly evolving. The trading significance of China's manufacturing industry or India's service industry was not a factor a decade ago. The exotic credit derivative instruments like CDO square structures did not exist before 2003. In 1985 the number of hedge funds was closer to one hundred, today they exceed 7,000. The market relationships, trading instruments, and changing participants keep introducing new variables. Besides the market-introduced variables, the hedge fund manager's intrinsic variables also keep changing. As hedge funds grow in size, they tend to saturate their strategies and tend to drift to other strategies. Additionally, with growth comes delegation of trading authority, this is inevitable. No single trader can be expected to effectively and single handedly manage billions of dollars in capital. An increase in size also leads to liquidity and anonymity issues, which yet introduce new variables into the returns equation. Therefore, I would argue that trying to perform statistical analysis on a hedge fund's historical returns to forecast future performance is very unscientific.

Some fund of funds will also look at a hedge fund's returns to determine the volatility and skew of the returns. Figure 7.1 shows the returns of hedge fund "A" with low steady returns, while Figure 7.2 shows the returns of hedge fund "B," which are a lot more volatile and exhibit fat tails. A fund

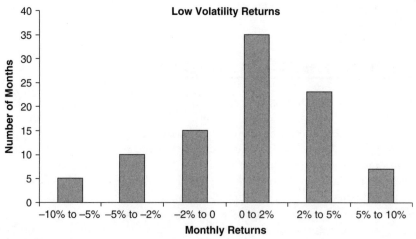

FIGURE 7.1 Hedge fund "A" returns.

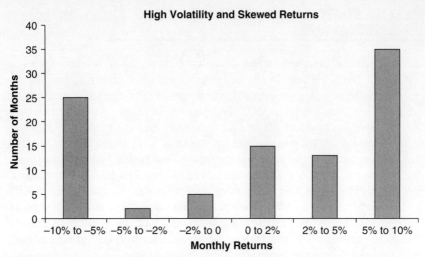

FIGURE 7.2 Hedge fund "B" returns.

of funds will prefer to pick hedge fund A over hedge fund B, even though the average monthly returns of hedge fund "A" are only 0.71 percent/month while that of hedge fund "B" are 1.18 percent/month. The fund of funds investor will attribute his decision to picking a hedge fund manager with a high Sharpe ratio.

$$\text{Sharpe Ratio} = \frac{\text{Annualized Returns} - \text{Risk Free Rate}}{\text{Volatility of Returns}}$$

Too many good strategies that generate alpha get passed over by the fund of funds because their return stream does not measure up to the academic and arbitrary standards established by the industry. On a Wall Street proprietary trading desk, the trading manager always stresses not just the importance of the results but how they were produced. Steady low-volatility returns over a short period might be a function of a rare trading opportunity or low-market volatility, just as high-volatility returns might be a function of trading in a high-volatility environment. Statistical analysis of a hedge fund's historical return stream at best is useless and at worst leads to a false sense of security. It definitely cannot be a substitute for digging deep into the strategy and truly understanding the return attributes by a qualified and experienced staff.

QUEST FOR STEADY RETURNS: SYSTEMATIC DESTRUCTION OF ALPHA

While we are on the topic of low-volatility returns, I want to dispel with the notion of steady returns in the hedge fund industry once and for all. The concept of steady returns over a long period of time does not exist. If you are gullible enough to have convinced yourself of such a concept, then there are plenty of Bernie Madoffs and KL Financials out there who will continue to take advantage of you. Before I proceed, I have to make an exception to my statement. There are very few and gifted hedge fund managers like Jim Simons and Steve Cohen who have managed to produce annualized returns in excess of 40 percent for the past fifteen years, but these funds are by and large closed to outside investors. The managers and their staff are the majority investors in their own funds. If I had the skill set to produce 40 percent returns year after year, why would I want to bother with managing anybody else's money either?

Volatility is a trader's friend. Figure 7.3 is a very simple example of the difference between a trader and a long-term investor.

Shown is a chart of the S&P 500 ETF, SPY, from January 2008 to January 2009. A long-term investor would buy the index in January 2008 and hold it through January 2009, thereby incurring a 34.6 percent loss (130 down to 85). But a trader would take advantage of the volatility and buy and sell the index several times over the same period of time as indicated by the B and S signals. One can see that from January 2008 to August 2008, the total number of signals was only six but as the market volatility increased, there were eleven signals from August 2008 to January 2009. The higher the number of such trading signals, the higher the chances of making money. In a perfect world, a trader would be able to capture all the above

FIGURE 7.3   Trader versus long-term investor.
Source: Charles Schwab & Co.

signals at the right time and produce steady profitable returns. But the reality is that most of the traders would only capture some of these signals and not at the perfect time, thereby most likely still producing positive returns but with high volatility.

When the industry preaches the need for steady returns, it forces a trader to become more conservative. The trader then would rather wait for trends in the marketplace than trade volatility. This eventually forces the trader's style and his returns to start to resemble more that of a long-term investor. Alpha, or excess market returns, gets destroyed, and the hedge fund investor is left with expensive beta, or market returns.

Some traders adopt other creative means of trying to generate steady returns. They will look for carry-type trades. A carry trade is one where the investor gets paid for sitting on a high coupon or high accrual position and prays that market volatility stays subdued, and he does not incur capital losses. Buying 10 percent coupon sub-prime bonds was such a carry trade. This strategy worked as long as the bonds did not default. Soon as the credit market seized up, the price of those bonds fell to almost ten cents on the dollar and instead of collecting a steady 10 percent coupon, the trader was left with a 90 percent loss on his position.

Selling option volatility and collecting premium is another such carry strategy. In the following example a trader might decide that the stock price of company "A" will not rise beyond $46 a share for the next three months. He decides to sell a call option on this stock at a strike of $46 and collect 1 percent in premium. As long as the stock price at maturity in three months stays below $46, the trader collects his steady 1 percent premium, but as the stock price starts rising, he starts to lose large amounts of money. This strategy is also termed "collecting pennies in front of a steamroller" and is shown in Figure 7.4.

Such carry strategies were very popular from 2004 to August 2007 when the market volatility was subdued and the need for high steady returns drove the hedge fund market to pile into carry trades. The market turmoil since August 2007 has basically led to an unwinding of these carry strategies and has been a major contributor to the massive destruction of wealth.

It seems that the real reason for investing in hedge funds has been lost. The search for alpha has brought not just the high net worth individuals but also the institutional players into the hedge fund industry. As discussed in Chapter 2, the need for returns has brought the pension funds and endowments to invest in the alternative space. But these investors have forgotten that high returns are commensurate with high volatility. By putting pressure on the hedge fund manager to produce steady returns, the hedge fund manager will start sacrificing big hits for risky singles. If you artificially try to

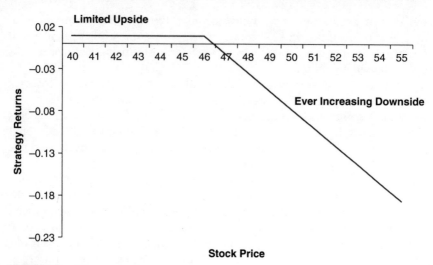

FIGURE 7.4 Carry strategy returns.

suppress volatility, over time the returns will eventually catch up with it and the investor will be left with nothing more than expensive beta or market returns.

BUCKETING BY ASSET CLASS AND GEOGRAPHY: A FLAWED CONCEPT

One of the benefits of investing in hedge funds through a fund of funds is diversification. Funds of funds theoretically invest across the spectrum of strategies to reduce the idiosyncratic risks arising from any single market sector. Several academic papers have published studies affirming that hedge funds are a separate asset class and that a fund of funds manager could reduce the volatility of his fund by implementing a systematic approach to fund of funds diversity. To achieve this, the funds of funds have created a bucketing system comprising the major strategies like long-short equity, relative value, global macro, and others. This strategy-based bucketing system is based on covering as many asset classes and geographies as possible. If you quiz a fund of funds manager, he will tell you that the performance of different asset classes and geographies is not correlated. Therefore, fund managers pick hedge funds that trade different asset classes and in different geographies, which should lead to a portfolio with lower volatility. Funds of funds will go to great lengths to ensure that they are not overweighted in any one particular strategy. Fairfield Greenwich Group, the now infamous fund of funds that invested and lost $7.5 billion with Madoff, said the following on its website: "Various hedge fund styles respond to changing market conditions in different ways. To reduce exposure to changing market conditions, FGG allocates to a diverse array of investment styles." It presented the following bucketing system on its website (Figure 7.5).

There are two problems with this approach. One, institutional capital flows looking for returns in times of low market volatility will drive up all asset classes in unison, and in times of duress, capital outflows will drive all asset classes down in unison as well, thereby providing little diversification benefits. Second, bucketing based on asset classes and geographies is a very mutual fund and beta approach to investing. It completely misses the point of alpha and hedge fund investing.

Let us explore these fallacies further. In the period between 2004 and August 2007 the global economic cycles were driven by a cheap credit environment. The Fed had kept interest rates low, leading to cheap and plentiful credit. The economy was humming along with the unemployment rate below 5 percent, the lowest in decades, and the consumer was feeling wealthy

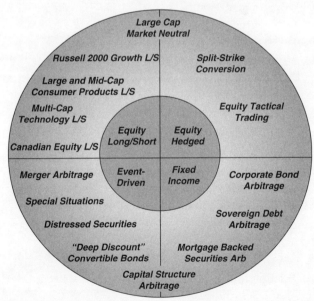

FIGURE 7.5 FGG bucketing system.
Source: www.fggus.com

as both the stock market and the real estate market were performing well. Consequently, U.S. consumer spending led to increased imports from the rest of the world, leading to a weaker U.S. dollar and strengthening foreign, especially emerging market, currencies. The foreign stock markets, especially the Asian stock markets, benefited from money inflows looking for even higher returns, owing to the higher economic growth rates than the United States. Increased world economic growth as well as investment into commodities saw a bull market in the commodities markets with oil reaching $147 per barrel. On the fixed income side, a search for yield led to a tightening in the bond credit spreads as well. Therefore, we saw that cheap credit and institutional capital flows searching for higher yields drove the global equity markets, real estate markets, and commodity markets higher in unison while driving the bond credit spreads lower and therefore corporate bond prices higher as well. As the money flows were coming out of the United States and going into global markets, we saw the U.S. dollar fall

TABLE 7.1 Performance of Hedge Fund Strategies

HFRX Index	2008 Total	2007 Total	2006 Total	2005 Total	2004 Total
HFRX Equal Weighted Strategies Index	(21.90)	3.97	8.83	1.28	2.72
HFRX Distressed Securities Index	(30.69)	3.99	9.56	1.21	8.95
HFRX Equity Hedge Index	(25.45)	3.21	9.23	4.19	2.18
HFRX Event Driven Index	(22.11)	4.88	10.32	2.81	6.93
HFRX Macro Index	5.61	3.19	5.61	6.67	(0.32)
HFRX Merger Arbitrage Index	3.69	4.85	10.73	3.72	2.80
HFRX Relative Value Arbitrage Index	(37.60)	5.80	10.65	(0.97)	1.98
HFRX Asia Composite Hedge Fund Index	(18.49)	17.27	10.06	21.25	6.98
	26.55	49.52	40.05	34.33	30.06
	49.52	40.05	34.33	30.06	24.8

Source: HedgeFundResearch.com

versus most of the global currencies. In the hedge fund world, buckets based on strategies such as equity long-short strategies, emerging market strategies, relative value strategies, and global macro all performed very well as is evident in Table 7.1.

The credit market blowup that started in August 2007 led to exactly the reverse flows as capital fled risky assets and came back to the safety of U.S. government bonds. This led to a drop in the global equity markets, real estate markets, commodity markets, and corporate bond prices. Commodity markets and the emerging market equity and currencies that had performed the best between 2004 and August 2007 fared the worst after the credit crisis started. The rush of money to the safety of the U.S. government bonds caused a rally in the U.S. dollar versus most of the global currencies. Consequently, the buckets created by the funds of funds based on asset classes and geographies performed poorly across the board. Where were the correlation benefits based on asset class and geographical bucketing?

ALPHA VERSUS BETA: THE TRADER GENERATES ALPHA, NOT THE STRATEGY

The terms alpha and beta are part of the Capital Asset Pricing Model (CAPM).

$$E(Ra) = Rf + Beta(E(Rm) - Rf)$$

Where $E(Ra)$ is the expected return of the asset "A"
    Rf is the risk-free rate
    $E(Rm)$ is the expected rate of return of the underlying market

Beta is a measure of how a security's volatility compares to the volatility in its underlying market. Therefore, a stock's beta measure would be derived from the stock market, e.g., S&P 500 or the NASDAQ. A beta of 1 indicates that the security's price volatility is the same as that of the market. A beta of less than 1 means that the security will be less volatile than the market while a beta of greater than 1 indicates that the security's price will be more volatile than the market.

Alpha is the excess return an asset provides when compared to the expected return from the CAPM model above. Therefore, if the expected return of an asset from the CAPM model above was 8 percent, but the asset returns 10 percent, then the alpha of that asset is 2 percent.

Almost every single underlying hedge fund strategy depends on one or a combination of several observable underlying markets. For example, a long-short equity strategy could be implemented on the stocks that make up the S&P 500 index. A relative value strategy could be a combination of a view on the direction of interest rate volatility and the direction of interest rates in Japan. A global macro strategy could be taking a view on the direction of the U.S. dollar versus the Asian currencies. Almost every hedge fund strategy, by definition, needs to be long some assets and short some other assets concurrently.

Therefore, the first important ingredient required to execute an alpha strategy in a market is the availability of means to short the market. If a market does not allow the strategy to be short some assets, then it would be impossible to implement a hedge fund strategy in that marketplace and more than likely the strategy's returns would be some form of beta. As long as the underlying market keeps trending in a particular direction, it will be very hard to determine the true composition of those returns. It is only when we see a prolonged downturn like the one in 2008 that the investor realizes the true beta measure of that strategy and therefore the correct amount of alpha.

A good example of this was seen in the Asian hedge fund strategies from 2004 to 2008. If, say, the Asian stock markets went up 50 percent the first year and then down 30 percent the following year, and the hedge fund that was trading these markets was up 75 percent the first year but then down 45 percent the next year, then that hedge fund would have not produced any alpha. The hedge fund would have just been levered one and a half times and the excess positive and negative returns would have been a function of a beta factor of 1.5. The hedge fund investor would have been much better off investing in an index fund or a mutual fund and creating his own leverage via a margin account. First, this would be much cheaper in terms of fees and, second, a lot more liquid. Index funds and mutual funds do not have redemption gates, and the liquidity periods are a lot more frequent than that of a hedge fund.

A closer look at the behavior of the funds of funds industry shows that this distinction between alpha and beta is often not understood. When I started raising capital for my Asia-focused hedge fund in 2003, most funds of funds did not understand the Asian markets and therefore did not have a bucket in their portfolios to invest in them. It was only after the boom in the Asian stock markets that the funds of funds became interested in Asia-focused hedge funds. Several Asian equity and debt-focused hedge funds cropped up that were basically long the Asian equity and debt markets while employing leverage. The tools for shorting stocks and bonds in Asia did not exist back then and rarely do even today in

TABLE 7.2 Comparing an Asia-Focused Hedge Fund Index with an ETF from 2004–2008

	2008	2007	2006	2005	2004
iShares MSCI Pacific ex-Japan Index (EPP)	−46%	24%	17%	14%	21%
HFRX Asia ex-Japan Index	−29%	40%	27%	11%	5%

Source: Reuters, www.hedgefundresearch.com

2009. As the Asian equity markets rallied, the funds of funds started investing with the Asia-focused hedge funds. Table 7.2 shows how the iShares MSCI Pacific ex-Japan Index (EPP) compares to the HFRX Asia ex-Japan hedge fund Index.

The comparison above clearly shows the high degree of correlation between the returns of the Asia-focused hedge funds with the MSCI Pacific Index, an exchange-traded fund. The correlation of the annual returns between the two is 87 percent. The returns of the HFRX Asia ex-Japan index look more like the returns of a long-only mutual fund, which is a form of beta and not alpha. An investor would have been much better off buying the ETF on margin rather than paying hefty fees and tying up his capital with the hedge funds focused on the Asian markets.

Besides the need for appropriate instruments, like ways to short a market, the second alpha concept to understand is that it is the trader who generates alpha and not the strategy. As a hedge fund investor, the key point to understand is that when investing in a hedge fund, you are investing with a group of traders and in their ability to generate alpha by trading the market through the up as well as down swings. The following are examples of a distinction between alpha and beta strategies.

Prolonged Bull or Bear Market

If an investor takes a bullish or bearish view on a market, then the best way to express that view is by utilizing a beta strategy, i.e., buying or selling ETFs. Examples of this could be the bull run in the Asian equities of 2004–2008 or the global rate cut cycle of 2008.

Markets with Short Cycles

It is extremely difficult to find markets where the level of conviction is high enough to establish long dated bullish or bearish positions. Most markets will tend to fluctuate and move in short bull or bear waves. Therefore, the best way to take advantage of this volatility is to invest with hedge fund managers who specialize at macroeconomic analysis or systematic models to be able to trade and capture these short-lived cycles.

Relative Value Markets

Inefficient markets can provide relative value opportunities. The relative value can occur between:

- Two instruments like a bond and a bond futures contract.
- Two stocks in the same sector, like Yahoo and Google.
- Two interrelated markets like the interest rates of two countries and the currency exchange rate between those two countries.
- Two or more instruments of different maturities, like the 2-year, 5-year, and 10-year bonds.

Market inefficiencies can occur due to the some of following reasons:

- Government interventions: For example, Central banks intervening in the currency markets to strengthen or weaken their currencies. This practice is quite common in developing countries.
- Corporate hedging issues: For example, corporates in a country issuing bonds and then engaging in interest rate hedging activity via derivatives. This asset liability hedging is quite common in most countries around the world.
- Government-controlled currency boards: For example, countries with currencies pegged to the U.S. dollar, like the Hong Kong Dollar or the Middle Eastern currencies.

It is almost impossible for the common investor to have the technical expertise to spot these relative value or arbitrage opportunities and establish strategies to make money off them. In these markets it is best to invest with hedge fund managers who specialize in relative value or arbitrage techniques and have experience in markets that exhibit these opportunities frequently. To successfully capture alpha in these markets, the hedge fund manager should possess both the technical skills as well as the experience of trading and understanding the flows affecting that market.

Specialized Strategies

Some hedge fund managers will have strategies that take advantage of very specialized markets that require considerable amount of relationship skills or an information network. An example of this is merger arbitrage. Such opportunities can only be identified as well as captured by managers with those specific skills.

This should show that bucketing on the basis of strategy or geography is not the correct approach to capturing alpha. It is always the trader and his skills that capture alpha and not a strategy bucket. Too many skilled hedge fund managers have been turned away by the fund of hedge funds industry because their strategy was thrown into a bucket that was out of favor at that point in time. Therefore, bucketing based on strategy is not only useless, but it also leads to a destruction of alpha as that hedge fund manager might never get a chance to prove his alpha generation skills due to a lack of capital.

The fund of funds investor needs to possess the skills to be able to identify markets as well as market cycles to adopt an alpha or a beta approach to investing. After the investor has determined the markets he or she wants to adopt an alpha approach to, he or she further needs to have the skills to determine if the hedge fund manager possesses the necessary skills and experience to be able to deliver that alpha. This due diligence does not stop with the initial allocation but needs to continue on a regular basis. Currently, the funds of funds do not possess the staff to be able to make that distinction. Therefore, they have adopted an asset class and geographical bucketing approach that results in mixing alpha with beta strategies—a very inefficient and expensive way of allocating capital.

10 PERCENT TO 20 PERCENT ALLOCATION RULE

Funds of hedge funds have placed investment caps on their hedge investments, such that they cannot be more than 20 percent of a hedge fund's total assets under management. Sometimes this number could be as low as 10 percent and in rare cases higher than 20 percent. Therefore, if a hedge fund has $100 million under management, the maximum a fund of funds will invest into it will be no more than $20 million. While this 10 to 20 percent number is quite random, it unequivocally demonstrates the tendency of herd mentality among fund of funds. A fund of funds will always ask a hedge fund manager about his other investors, and it wants to hear some of the big and common names in the industry. Investing alongside some of the bigger names in the industry provides the fund of funds manager with a "job hedge." The CIO of the fund of funds has very little faith in his own due diligence so he relies on the safety in numbers approach and the "club effect" to offset the blame if something were to go wrong. Like a herd of wildebeest, the fund of funds feels more secure if he is not the only investor in a hedge fund and has other well-known members of the community invested with him. This gives him the excuse of, "Yes, I messed up, but so did Johnny and he is so much bigger than me."

A fund of funds will claim that by not being a majority investor in a hedge fund it is protecting its ability to get its capital out if something goes wrong with the hedge fund. There is very little rationality behind this claim. In normal times, an investor can redeem any and all capital at the stated redemption periods. In volatile times, like 2008, when a hedge fund erects its redemption gates, whether an investor is 100 percent of a hedge fund's capital or 10 percent, the effect would still be the same. When the gates are erected, an investor is limited not by the dollar amount but by a percentage amount of capital that he can redeem at any given time. Therefore, if an investor has $50 million invested in a hedge fund and the gate restricts redemptions to 25 percent, then it will still take the investor four redemption periods to fully get his capital out. It is immaterial whether the hedge fund size was $50 million or $500 million. All costs and fees would still be charged on a pro-rata basis on the capital over the redemption period.

The risk of fewer investors in a hedge fund lies more with the hedge fund manager than the investor. This is because every investor represents a bigger chunk of the hedge fund manager's assets, and it could severely affect the fees and capital if any of those investors were to redeem. Being a majority investor in fact can give the fund of funds more control and say over a hedge fund's operation. Funds of funds should love the opportunity of being early investors into a hedge fund and in return bargaining for special privileges. An educated fund of funds that understands a hedge fund manager's strategy should ask for complete transparency and favorable liquidity terms. Complete transparency will allow the fund of funds to effectively perform its ongoing due diligence and ensure that the hedge fund manager is sticking to his strategy and risk parameters. Favorable liquidity terms will also ensure that if the hedge fund manager strays from his strategy or steps outside the risk parameters often, thereby putting the investor's capital at undue risk, the fund of funds can redeem its investment.

A skilled fund of funds investor would always want as much transparency and information on his hedge fund investment and would therefore use his ability to invest early and in as large a size as possible to get that control. Unfortunately, most funds of funds do not have the expertise to understand the strategies or risk management practices of the hedge funds that they invest in; therefore, they adopt a "safety in numbers" approach and random allocation caps of 10 to 20 percent.

MANAGING A HEDGE FUND MANAGER

To understand how to properly manage a hedge fund investment, it is very crucial to understand how a hedge fund manager has been managed throughout his career. As described before, a hedge fund manager starts out as a trader on a Wall Street proprietary trading desk. While he is a junior trader, his every move is being watched by some senior trader on the desk. He rarely has decision-making authority, and when he does, he works with very tight stop losses. If the junior trader violates those risk management guidelines one too many times, he does not survive to execute another trade. When that trader becomes a senior trader and is given his own capital to trade, he is still being monitored by either the head of the desk or the risk management group. Every trade that is executed is then monitored and accounted for independently by the bank, and it is the bank's middle office that generates the daily valuations and profit and loss statements. When that senior trader starts to run up losses on a position, he gets hounded by the senior management or the risk department people several times a day. They check his convictions on his trade and either make him adhere to the risk management guidelines or in rare cases give him slight leeway. The trader discusses his portfolio usually at a weekly meeting of peers or with the head of the department. Based on the dialogue at the meeting, the trader might decide to increase the size of some positions, cut some existing positions, or even delay the execution of any new positions. After the losses taken by some of the proprietary trading desks in the last decade, rarely is a trader allowed to trade in a cocoon. He is under constant supervision by the risk department, head of desks, or head of divisions, and even at the most senior level, by supervision by the management committees. Therefore, it is very essential to take even a proprietary trader's track record with a grain of salt as it is almost impossible that those returns were generated with no outside influence or supervision.

Now we take this very successful trader out of the proprietary trading desk of a bank and put him in a hedge fund. Given the current level of expertise in the allocation industry and therefore the lack of oversight, it is fair to say that the hedge fund trader does start to trade in a cocoon. When that trader was allocated capital at a bank, it came with rigorous guidelines and constant monitoring by other seasoned professionals in the trading and risk management fields. But now that same trader gets allocated several times more capital by the CIO of a fund of funds, who has usually not even spent a day trading proprietary capital or managing traders. When a driver goes from driving 65 miles an hour on a U.S. highway to the unregulated Autobahns of Germany, accidents are bound to happen even with the most seasoned drivers.

BOOKRUNNER VERSUS A PROPRIETARY TRADER

While most hedge fund managers who launch their funds have gone through the rigorous process of getting the right education and, spending years on a Wall Street proprietary trading desk under the tutelage of a rabbi, there have been several funds launched by managers with no proprietary trading background. Some of these were bookrunners or market makers, some equity analysts, and some even traditional long-only equity managers with no experience in generating alpha on a defined amount of capital. Yet their hedge fund strategies expounded all the facets of a long-short equity hedge fund, and they managed to get funded as well.

The distinction between a bookrunner or market maker and a proprietary trader is often not understood, so I will devote a few paragraphs to outline the major differences. A bookrunner is also a trader, but his main job is to hedge out the risk in the bank's client orders portfolio. The bookrunner makes money by making sure that the cost of executing and hedging the order is lower than the price charged from the bank's client. This role becomes more and more complex with the nature of the client's order. If it is a simple stock order, then the bookrunner's challenge is in being able to source enough liquidity to fill the order, but if it is a complex long-maturity derivative transaction, then the cost of hedging over the life of the trade can be a lot more involved. A bookrunner also takes views on the market and has a responsibility that is a hybrid between a risk manager and a proprietary trader. Every client order generates market information and comes with a profit margin for the bookrunner. A bookrunner takes advantage of that market information and makes a living by trying to preserve most of that profit margin. A bookrunner additionally also has access to theoretically unlimited capital. If a client order generates enough risk that needs to be carried in the bank's books, the bookrunner can ask for and usually will receive access to additional capital from the bank's balance sheets. This decision is usually incumbent on the potential profit opportunity that can be generated from the client order. Conversely, if the client order flow is minimal, the bookrunner does not have to utilize the capital to generate profits, in which case his capital allocation gets reduced. Given this floating capital concept, an investor should be very cautious in determining a bookrunner's profitability, as it is hard to ascertain the amount of capital utilized in generating that profit. A $50 million profit in a year looks impressive, but not if it was generated by buying and holding $1 billion of one-year T-bills at a 5 percent interest rate. A proprietary trader, on the other hand, does not have the benefit of market information or the profit margin generated by a client order. He pretty much sits in a corner of the trading floor and generates profit by analyzing data and news and taking prudent positions with his defined capital base. A hedge fund manager's training ground is a proprietary trader's seat at a Wall Street bank and not that of a bookrunner's. But often this distinction is lost on a wide-eyed analyst at a fund of funds with a stack of papers with preprinted questions in front of him.

SO-CALLED HEDGE FUND EXPERTS

The hedge fund investing community is filled with so called hedge fund experts. These experts range from fund of funds, consultants, marketers, and newsletter editors to professors writing academic papers galore on how to best perform due diligence on a hedge fund manager and how to construct a portfolio of hedge fund strategies. I have always wondered what makes these people experts in hedge funds. The number one thing to understand about hedge funds is the strategies they employ and how they manage their risk. Operational and legal due diligence, while important, is a distant second to strategy due diligence, as the strategy and risk due diligence has to be performed constantly throughout the investment period.

The people who are qualified to perform strategy and risk level due diligence would be classified as the hedge fund experts. The only people who can understand the strategies, how they are constructed and implemented, their pitfalls and challenges, are the people who have experience trading these strategies first-hand. I am sure 99 percent of the fund of funds community will disagree with me, so here are some analogies to better illustrate my point:

- Most top coaches of a NFL franchise are ex-players themselves. Question is, when the franchise wants to recruit new talent does it send stadium builders, groundskeepers, and concession stand employees to do the scouting or coaches themselves?
- After a few years, a car salesman could write a book on the benefits of owning a Honda versus a Ford versus a BMW. Question is, if you blow the transmission, would you take your car to the salesman or to an auto mechanic?
- Lawyers have built very lucrative practices suing doctors for medical malpractice. After a few years, these lawyers probably understand the medical profession extremely well and are well versed in a lot of the medical terminology as well. Question is, Would you ask a lawyer to pick the perfect specialist for your illness or would you seek the help of your general practitioner?

I can give countless examples from just about every walk of life that will illustrate my point that expertise in a particular field is gained by actually performing that very task itself and not by observing or servicing it from the sidelines. But in the world of hedge fund investing, the paradigm is different. Here, if you want to invest your money with hedge fund traders, you hire management consultants, lawyers, relationship managers, and salesman to pick traders. I definitely do not understand the logic behind these decisions, but I can speculate and a few reasons come to mind.

First, the distinction between an asset raiser and an asset investor at a fund of funds has been lost. Funds of funds have been started by relationship managers and salesmen with excellent global contacts with the high net worth community. While they have excellent client relationship skills and are capable of raising a lot of capital, they lack the understanding of how to best invest this capital. The funds of funds have adopted a (flawed) statistics based model to investing, with very little understanding of the actual investment strategies. So far, they have not been held accountable by their end investors, but given the poor performance of 2008 combined with the scandals, a lot of questions should and will be asked of the funds of funds industry. Hopefully, this will show that the funds of funds are experts at raising capital but lack the expertise to effectively deploy it across hedge fund strategies.

The second reason I can think of is the difficulty in attracting and retaining trading experts. The number of good traders in the industry is small. Very few traders survive the Darwinian process to amass ten years or more of market trading experience. Given the compensation economics of trading, most of these good traders prefer to trade at a Wall Street bank or at a hedge fund. Therefore, the funds of funds have been forced to fill the allocator seats with market observers rather than market practitioners.

The third reason for the proliferation of the so-called hedge fund experts has clearly been the rich rewards for serving the hedge fund industry. The fund of funds fee structure of 1 percent annual management fees and 10 percent performance fees has created a multibillion-dollar industry for the middleman. This has attracted a lot of self-professed experts who have little or no industry experience and are solely there to get a ride on the gravy train. We have seen this phenomenon several times in history from the automobile industry boom of the early twentieth century to the Internet craze of the late twentieth century.

As the hedge fund industry matures and the investors demand true value-added expertise from the fund of funds, we should see the industry change its model and hire true experts with years of trading and risk management experience to handle capital allocation functions.

HEDGE FUNDS: HOUSE OF SECOND OR THIRD CHANCES?

John Meriwether

1998: John Meriwether and his group of traders incur a $4.5 billion loss and their hedge fund Long Term Capital Management goes bust.

1999: John Meriwether and a lot of the traders from Long Term Capital Management launch a second hedge fund firm called JWM Partners.

2008: JWM Partners ran Relative Value Opportunity Fund II, a $1.6 billion fund, racked up forty percent losses and decided to shut down the fund.

2009: Rumor has it that John Meriwether wants to launch a third fund.

Brian Hunter

2003: Joins Deutsche Bank's energy desk. His wide profit and loss swings provoked a stormy face-off with superiors.

December 2003: In a single week, his group loses over $50 million.

February 2004: His supervisors lock him out of the trading system and make him an analyst.

April 2004: Hunter leaves Deutsche Bank and joins Amaranth Capital as a trader.

September 2006: Amaranth loses $6 billion or 65 percent of the fund's capital on Hunter's single natural gas trade.

2007: Hunter launches Solengo Capital, a commodity investment vehicle.

December 2008: Deutsche Bank Credit Desk

Deutsche Bank, Germany's largest bank, reported that it lost $5 billion in 2008—including $1.8 billion from its credit trading desk. The losses by the credit desk exceed the estimated $1.5 billion in profits the group generated in 2006 and 2007 combined.

January 2009: The head of the credit desk leaves Deutsche Bank to start his own hedge fund.

January 2009

> Several multibillion dollar hedge funds suffered losses exceeding 50 percent in 2008, but announced plans to raise capital for new funds.

Stories like this are quite frequent on Wall Street. A trader's career life expectancy is low on Wall Street, thus the need for outsized compensation packages in profitable years. In the years gone by, before the hedge fund industry took off, losing money on Wall Street was considered the worst sin a trader could commit. If a trader lost a lot of money, he rarely got another job at a Wall Street trading desk. At that point he generally accepted a managerial job, changed professions, or retired. But it seems now that the paradigm has changed. If you lose a lot of money on a trading desk or blow up a fund, you can always start your own hedge fund. As long as you have a good enough excuse and can lay off the blame on other traders, your bosses, conniving market conspirators, or just bad luck, you would find some fund of funds that would gladly give you a second chance.

WHY DOES A LOSING HEDGE FUND MANAGER SHUT DOWN HIS FUND?

Once a hedge fund manager is down a lot, like 40 percent or greater, he loses the incentive to keep running that fund due to the high water mark clause. The high water mark clause states that the manager would have to make back the entire loss before he can start collecting the lucrative 20 percent incentive fees again. Therefore, the most economical decision for the hedge fund manager is to shut down that fund and start a new fund where he is automatically set at ground zero and can start collecting incentive fees on any new profits he generates. The hedge fund investors are a lot more forgiving than the management at Wall Street trading desks and will often give that hedge fund manager a second or even third chance.

WHY DOES THE INDUSTRY KEEP FUNDING A FAILED TRADER?

I have often grappled with the reasoning for why the failed trader or the failed hedge fund manager keeps getting funded a second or even a third time by the fund of funds industry. The logic behind the decision making escapes me, but I can speculate on the possible reasons for the irrational reasoning.

1. First, it is probably reputation and relationships. One of the first lessons I learned upon joining Wall Street was that it is a very small community

and a very clubby place. Most of the top executives are represented from a handful of top business schools in the country. By graduating from one of these top institutions, you become a member of the fraternity. The high stress environment and the physical proximity of working on a trading floor create a sense of camaraderie that can last a lifetime. Job security and therefore loyalty are alien concepts, so you find people changing jobs within the firm and across firms with a very high regularity. Thus, after spending several years at a bank's trading desk, a trader often develops a widespread network across the financial industry. When a successful trader leaves to start a hedge fund, he takes his reputation and all the benefits of his network with him. It is likely that this reputation and relationship network often end up trumping due diligence parameters. But as I have illustrated in Chapter 1, the number one lesson to be learned from observing the patterns in the various scandals is that relationships should not trump due diligence. It can often prove very costly, sometimes to the tune of $65 billion, as in the case of Bernie Madoff.

2. The second likely reason why failed hedge fund managers get funded is most likely investor gullibility and their success in selling one of the excuses, blaming other traders, bosses, conniving market conspirators, or just bad luck. The true reason a trader loses a lot of money at a trading desk or at a hedge fund has nothing to do with market conspiracies or bad luck. It has all to do with poor risk management and a breakdown of basic trader discipline. Risk management problems are easier to fix than trader discipline problems. A hedge fund manager can always hire a competent and strong risk manager who with the help of appropriate technology will make sure that the fund's risk stays within defined parameters and stop loss limits are followed diligently. He would have the final say and would not be overridden by the Chief Investment Officer, who generally is the hedge fund manager himself.

   The second problem, breakdown of trader discipline, is a much harder problem to fix. Discipline is part of a person's character, be it in trading or in life. How a person balances greed and fear, how he manages his own ego, how secure he is in his own convictions, and his willingness to accept his faults cannot be imbued overnight. They are learned over a lifetime. Therefore, if a trader has lost his discipline once, he most likely will lose it again. This is a very important lesson for a fund of funds investor to understand and keep in mind before he decides to fund another manager who has lost his trading discipline and shown a weakness in his character.

3. Third, selective memory. Often, a failed hedge fund manager or a Wall Street trader will launch his second or third venture with his own

capital and perhaps some from friends and family. It is only human nature to tread very carefully once you have taken a nasty fall. Therefore,
the manager in his new venture will do his analysis to pick out the best
trade ideas, apply rigorous risk management principles, and post strong
and steady returns for a period of time. It is only after he has built a new
six-month to one-year solid track record that he will aggressively begin
marketing his fund again to the same investors who got burned the first
time. Another facet of human nature is that we are forgiving souls and
want to believe in the good of a person and sweep the bad under the
carpet. Therefore, when the same hedge fund manager approaches the
investors with mea culpa about the previous venture, promises of doing
it better a second time, and backed by a strong track record, it is very
likely that the investors will reinvest with that manager again.

CONCLUSION

In the above sections, I have shown some of the core problems with the
existing fund of funds investment methodology. To recap:

1. Evaluating a hedge fund based on historical data is at best useless and at
   worst provides a false sense of security.
2. Asking a hedge fund to produce steady low-volatility returns will only
   lead to destruction of true alpha-producing strategies.
3. Bucketing hedge fund strategies by asset class and geographies does not
   provide correlation benefits and is not the way to evaluate hedge fund
   strategies.
4. The distinction between alpha and beta strategies is lost. A trader generates alpha, not the strategy.
5. Limiting an investment to 10 to 20 percent of a hedge fund manager's
   total assets under management shows a lack of conviction in due diligence and a reliance on safety in numbers approach.
6. Funds of funds often do not know how to make the distinction between
   analysts, long-only managers, bookrunners, and proprietary traders.
7. To properly manage a hedge fund investment, fund of funds CIOs need
   to be experienced traders and trading managers themselves.
8. Throwing good capital after bad has turned the hedge fund industry to
   a house of second or even third chances.

There should be little doubt left in the mind of the reader that given the
current setup of the fund of funds industry and a lack of expertise, incidents
like Bernie Madoff, KL Financial, Bayou Capital, Long Term Capital

Management, Amaranth Advisors, etc. will continue to happen in the future as well. After the recent scandals, it will be disappointing if the fund of funds are permitted to hide behind a defense that many investors, some even more "sophisticated" than them, were fooled. It is quite evident that the funds of funds do not possess the requisite expertise and are following a flawed model to do their job. They have not done what they are paid to do and, worst of all, what in their marketing pitches they advocated they would do. The biggest cop out would be to hide behind legal disclosures, which is exactly what Tremont recently did after losing $3 billion in the Bernie Madoff scandal. "We believe the firm's disclosures were adequate and fully complied with all legal requirements," Mr. Illingworth, the Tremont spokesman, said.

Another classic example of this hypocrisy is Sandra Manzke, the principal partner at Maxam Capital Management in Darien, Connecticut, and a former head of alternative investments at Tremont who helped set up some of the early Madoff feeder funds there. In a November 2008 letter to her investors, she said that she was "appalled and disgusted by a dearth of integrity in the hedge fund industry. There are too many bad apples for my taste, and it only takes a few to bring the industry to its knees." Perhaps her letter to her investors was a prophecy or maybe an admission of guilt as she gladly collected fees while directing the entire $280 million of her client's money to Madoff. Maxam Capital Management shut down in December 2008.

CHAPTER 8

Remodeling the Funds of Hedge Funds

In the previous chapters I have outlined the reasons that have led to the failure of the so-called experts, funds of hedge funds. Now I will address a brand new approach to investing in hedge funds and how a fund of funds should be structured and managed. There is a lot of wealth in the world that is eagerly watching the alternative investment space of hedge funds but does not have the expertise to properly evaluate these investments. The recent newspaper headlines about failed due diligence on part of the funds of hedge funds have not helped foster any sense of confidence either. When the industry experts that the investors rely on to conduct due diligence on the hedge funds get duped, it only pushes capital further away from hedge funds. In fact, the hedge fund industry has shrunk by close to 40 percent from the end of 2007 to January of 2009. The fund of funds industry needs to change its model, the approach to hedge fund investing, if it wants to gain the respect and backing of the high net worth community, the institutional clientele, as well as the hedge funds it invests in. A properly designed fund of funds can be a very useful allocation conduit in the hedge fund industry that can also justify the additional layer of fees it charges.

FIVE INVIOLABLE COMMANDMENTS

Before we get into the proper way of conducting strategy-level due diligence, a hedge fund needs to have the following infrastructure in place before even the thought of an investment can be entertained. I call them the five inviolable commandments:

1. An independent industry-recognized auditor.
2. An independent industry-recognized administrator/custodian.

3. Trade execution via independent entities, like prime brokers.
4. Fund valuations conducted independently by a third party, like an administrator.
5. A hedge fund manager who is willing to talk at length and in depth about his strategy and provide regular risk and return reporting.

The above ingredients will ensure the required transparency and veracity of the information coming out of a hedge fund. Once the above ingredients are in place, then begins the true due diligence, the strategy-level due diligence, by a fund of funds.

TRADERS MANAGING TRADING INVESTMENTS

Funds of funds desperately need to understand the importance of not just raising assets but also deploying them effectively. To ensure this, they need to separate the asset-raising function from the asset-investing section. Asset raising requires client relationship skills and experience acquired on the institutional sales desks of Wall Street banks and the private client departments that deal with the global high net worth and institutional community. Currently, the funds of funds have a plethora of asset raisers. Effective asset deployment in the hedge fund industry can only be done by trading managers who have been practitioners on Wall Street trading desks for several years. Currently, the funds of funds do not have asset deployers. A significant amount of time and money needs to be invested on the asset-investing section if the fund of funds community wants to truly fulfill its obligations to its investors.

An investment in a hedge fund is an investment in a group of traders and their trading strategy. Therefore, the asset-investment division of a fund of funds needs to mimic a proprietary trading desk of a Wall Street bank. The division needs to be run by a panel of senior traders who have amassed years of experience on Wall Street trading desks, first trading various strategies and second managing other traders who have run these strategies as well. Given the wide variety of trading strategies in the hedge fund universe, it will be very difficult to find one trading manager who has experience in all these strategies. Therefore, the best approach is to assemble a panel of trading experts and concentrate on investing in only those strategies that match the expertise of this panel.

Most of the hedge fund strategies these days employ leverage and are executed using exchange traded as well as OTC (over-the-counter) derivative instruments. Therefore, the trading managers need to be assisted by risk managers who are proficient in assessing not just linear but also nonlinear risk in the portfolios as well. Currently, every fund of funds insists on regular reporting of returns. Funds of funds ask hedge funds for a daily estimate of the returns, but how come no fund of funds asks for regular risk reporting as well? As any seasoned trader will tell you, risk and returns go hand in hand. By just looking at the returns and not the risk, you are only getting half the picture. The key component of how those returns were generated is more important than the returns themselves. The funds of funds would have to insist on not just regular return reporting, but risk reporting as well. This task is easier than it seems and can be accomplished without too much encumbrance on part of the hedge fund manager. There are several third-party service providers that can get the positions of a hedge fund directly from its administrator. These service providers can then translate the positions into formatted risk reports with multiple levels of risk parameters. These risk reports can then be furnished to any and all of the hedge fund's investors.

DIFFERENTIATE BETWEEN ALPHA AND BETA STRATEGIES

This panel of senior trading managers will have the expertise to understand the market dynamics and thus what type of strategies would thrive in that market as well. An investor makes money one of the following three ways in any given market:

1. **Mean Reversion Strategies:** Generally, after a period of volatility that can be caused by a number of factors ranging from massive institutional money flows, market news, to position liquidations, prices of securities might deviate from their true intrinsic value. Mean reversion refers to the movement of the security price back to that intrinsic value. This type of strategy is often adopted by a lot of relative value managers as well as global macro funds, distressed securities funds, and special situation funds as well.
2. **Momentum-Based Strategies:** The second way an investor makes money in a market is by following a trend. These trends can be short lived with durations of a few weeks or very long, lasting like the Internet boom or the Asian equity market boom. This type of strategy is quite popular with global macro funds and long-short hedge funds as well.
3. **Carry Trade Strategies:** As the name suggests, carry trade strategies involve selling option premiums or buying high yielding assets and financing them with short-term cheap borrowings. Carry-trade strategies thrive in a market with cheap credit and low volatility.

Each of the abovementioned strategies has a time and place based on the economic cycle. Some of these strategies can be executed on a long-only basis, especially the long-duration, momentum-based strategies, by buying ETFs, while some require the expertise of a hedge fund manager's proprietary trading methodology.

The investing panel's responsibility will be to identify the markets in which long-only or beta strategies should be executed and then pick hedge fund managers for the remaining pure alpha strategies. The fund of funds should run a trading group of its own whose responsibility would be to execute these beta-only strategies. By executing their own beta strategies, the fund of funds will not be paying hedge fund fees for market-directional strategies and will not be competing with the hedge fund managers on pure alpha strategies, either.

BUCKETING BASED ON TRADER METHODOLOGY

In the previous chapter I explained why bucketing based on asset class or geography does not provide any real diversification benefits. Additionally, it is the hedge fund trader who produces alpha and not the strategy. Therefore, it makes sense to bucket hedge funds based on hedge fund manager's trading style, e.g., long volatility, positive carry, systematic or high frequency, momentum, arbitrage, or some combination thereof. These trading styles are very distinct from each other, and they would provide true correlation benefits irrespective of the market cycle, asset class, or geography that they are implemented in.

In Table 8.1, I have listed some of the popular trading styles that hedge fund managers implement, like mean reversion, positive carry, and others. The next section of the table discusses the source of risk to these styles. Assuming that the hedge fund manager performs competent research on the trade ideas, the market parameter that can upend even the best research is market volatility. Sudden volatility shocks are indicative of new information in the marketplace that was previously unaccounted for in the trade analysis. Generally, volatility spikes in one asset class or geography will affect other asset classes and geographical markets as well. Most strategies would not perform well in a volatility shock scenario unless they were complemented with low-probability option protection schemes. Steadily rising volatility or falling volatility will have different effects on different trading methodologies.

The next section of this table illustrates the source of returns for the various trading strategies. The source of returns for any strategy is either capital gains or positive carry. I have indicated the approximate portion of

TABLE 8.1 Popular Hedge Fund Trading Styles

Trading Style	Risk			Source of Returns		Position Duration
	Volatility Shock	Rising Volatility	Falling Volatility	Carry	Capital Gains	
Mean Reversion	Mixed	Mixed	Mixed	50%	50%	Medium to Long
Positive Carry	Negative	Negative	Positive	80%	20%	Long
Systematic or High Frequency	Mixed	Positive	Negative	1%	99%	Short
Momentum	Negative	Negative	Positive	20%	80%	Short to Medium

the returns that can be attributed to both capital gains and positive carry, per strategy.

Finally, position duration or the position holding period for the various strategies also differs. The classifications of short, medium, and long are very relative measures. Short durations can be as short as a few seconds, especially for high-frequency trading, and long can be as long as a year or longer for some of the relative value methodologies. I will go into further detail on each of the trading strategies/methodologies that I have mentioned in the following sections.

Mean Reversion

As explained earlier, mean reversion refers to the movement of the security price back to its intrinsic value. This type of strategy is often adopted by a lot of relative value managers as well as funds that trade in the global macro space, distressed securities funds, and special situation funds. Mean-reversion-type strategies can have a mixed response to periods of volatility. Let us examine two examples to determine the effect of volatility on mean-reversion-type strategies. From the end of 2004 to July 2007, the high yielding global currencies like the U.S. dollar kept rallying against the Japanese yen due to a multitude of reasons, the large interest rate differential between the two countries being one of them. Credit was easily available and market volatility was falling to ever-lower levels. This led to a proliferation of carry trades, where asset purchases around the world were financed by borrowings in Japanese yen. The investing community was keenly aware that on a valuation basis, USD/JPY exchange rate had moved quite far from its true intrinsic level. Since July 2007 the USD/JPY exchange rate has corrected almost 30 percent and thereby reverted closer to its true intrinsic level. In this example, USD/JPY exchange rate drifted away from its mean in a period of falling volatility and reverted back to its mean after a volatility shock and the subsequent period of rising volatility.

As a second example let us look at the credit spreads of highly rated corporations in the United States. Since July 2007 credit spreads on highly rated corporate bonds have blown out to very high levels due to a lack of credit arising from the credit crisis. Valuation measures would suggest that these levels are far from their true intrinsic levels and will soon revert. In this example, a volatility shock resulted in the credit spreads moving away from their mean, and a period of falling volatility will see them revert back to their mean.

Therefore, mean reversion strategies can perform in a low- or a high-volatility environment. Depending on how these strategies are implemented, the returns could be a combination of carry and capital gains. As mean reversion takes time, the holding period of these strategies can range from a few weeks to a few months.

Positive Carry

Positive carry strategies involve selling expensive option premium and buying high yielding assets and financing them with short-term cheap borrowings. Carry-trade strategies thrive in a market with falling volatility as we saw from 2004 to July 2007. Volatility shocks or periods of rising volatility are bad for positive carry strategies. As the name suggests, the source of returns for these strategies will generally come from carry and very little from capital gains. But sometimes if the market as a whole is chasing the same positive carry strategies, for example, long USD versus short JPY—then some of the strategy gains can come from capital gains as well. Positive carry strategies tend to be longer in duration as the length of the holding period is directly proportional to the amount of carry gains.

Systematic or High Frequency

Systematic or high frequency trading strategies are driven by computer algorithms and tend to capture small price moves several times a day on a variety of liquid markets around the world. For these strategies to thrive, they require a lot of price movement, i.e., volatility in the markets. Extended periods of little or no price movement will mean that there will be fewer trading opportunities for these strategies to capture. Volatility shocks will have a mixed reaction on these strategies as well. Volatility shocks will generally introduce new variables into the markets that might not be accounted for in the existing computer algorithms. Furthermore, these new variables might not be driven by any logical patterns and may not have been present in any previous market cycle either. It might take the computer algorithms time to adjust to these new variables to be able to predict future price movements; in some cases, they might never be able to adjust. Therefore, the effect of volatility shocks is at best mixed on the systematic or high-frequency trading methodology. In systematic trading, holding periods are very short, thus the name high frequency, sometimes as short as a few seconds, and nearly all of the gains are from capital gains. This trading methodology is unlike any other in the hedge fund universe and will tend to provide uncorrelated returns for the fund of funds portfolio. Additionally, as every computer-trading algorithm will differ in methodology, frequency, and underlying markets, there are good chances that the returns among the various systematic trading programs will also have low correlation to each other.

Momentum

The physics definition of momentum is the product of the mass of a body and the velocity with which it is traveling. Markets will exhibit a similar behavior and trend in a particular direction for a period of time. As the mass of this system increases—that is, more capital and players get involved in the trend—the trade's momentum will increase. Momentum methodologies rely on the trend to continue undisturbed for as long as possible. Therefore, volatility shocks are not good for existing momentum trades. Volatility shocks usually end the existing momentum trades and give rise to new ones. Rising or falling volatility will have different effects on a momentum trade depending on the age of the trade. If the momentum trade is young, it implies that the market has taken a new direction. As more players hit their stop losses and exit old trends to join the new momentum, trade volatility in that market will generally be on the rise. As the momentum trade ages and continues in the same direction undisturbed, the underlying market's volatility will generally start to fall. Momentum traders tend to make most of their returns from price movements or capital gains, although trade construction might give rise to some positive carry returns as well. Momentum trades are executed by global macro funds and long-short equity funds quite often, and the holding periods of these trades can be anywhere from a few weeks to a few years. Generally, the longer a momentum trade runs, the more it starts to look like a long-only beta trade. The fund of funds investment panel's challenge will be in deciding which trends can run for a long time and establish those as beta trades through ETFs and delegate the other shorter momentum strategies to the alpha managers, i.e., hedge funds.

APPROPRIATE RISK TEMPLATE BY STRATEGY

Once the hedge fund managers are bucketed by trading methodologies to create a truly diversified and uncorrelated portfolio, the fund of funds investment panel's real job begins. A trader on Wall Street is hired based on his education, expertise, and proven track record, but his capital allocation and tenure is determined by his superior's ongoing due diligence. In the hedge fund industry, the funds of funds are the trader's bosses, and they need to start acting like it as well. Questions about adherence to risk limits and ensuring no style drift in the preprinted AIMA due diligence questionnaire carry very little weight. You might as well ask the hedge fund manager if he intends to steal your money and run away; the answers to both these questions is obvious. It is the fund of funds' responsibility to monitor the risk as well as returns of the hedge fund manager on a regular basis to ensure that risk parameters are followed and there is no style drift.

Every strategy and methodology is unique and therefore has its own set of risk parameters. Therefore, one set of risk questions across all strategies will cover no more than half of the actual risk in the portfolio. Risk templates need to be developed that capture all the first-order, second-order, and third-order risks of a strategy and need to be tailored to that particular strategy. To explain my point further, I have presented an example of a portfolio with positions in currencies and interest rates of various countries around the world. The hypothetical portfolio below highlights risks that can arise from a portfolio that utilizes derivative securities as well as certain systematic risks inherent in an emerging markets portfolio. The example below is just a glimpse into the possible risks inherent in a hedge fund portfolio; to understand and decipher all the possible pitfalls will require considerable amount of trading and risk management experience on part of the investor. The following section requires understanding of certain risk management principles and derivatives instruments, so is targeted more toward the industry practitioners. Therefore, even if the reader decides to skip this portion, he or she should make sure that the investment advisor handling his or her hedge fund investments does have a thorough understanding and, more important, experience in the material covered in the following sections.

Hypothetical Interest Rate Risk Report

Figure 8.1 is a sample risk report of the interest rate risk in a portfolio. The first section captures the linear or the delta risk in the portfolio. This risk is represented as the profit or loss for a one basis point move in interest rates of a particular country.

- The report is broken out by the various countries that the fund trades in, that is, United States, Australia, New Zealand, South Korea and Hong Kong.
- A positive number indicates a profit and a negative number a loss.
- All the numbers for other countries are converted into U.S. dollars.
- Portfolio SUM is the addition of all the risk numbers, positive and negative.
- Absolute SUM is the addition of all the absolute risks, assuming no correlation benefits.
- Swap vs. Futures captures the basis risk between two different instruments. The portfolio might be long swaps and short bond futures in the same amount. Even though this position would show a net delta risk of zero, the basis risk on this position would be quite large.
- Similarly, Swap vs. Bonds is the basis risk between the swaps and the cash bonds.

The second section illustrates the second-order risk in the portfolio arising from the interest rate options portfolio.

INTEREST RATE RISK							
Delta Risk	**Portfolio SUM**	**Absolute SUM**	**USD**	**AUD**	**NZD**	**KRW**	**HKD**
SUM [0 - 2Yr]	($4,000)	$74,000	$20,000	$10,000	$5,000	($35,000)	($4,000)
SUM [2.1Yr - 5Yr]	($2,300)	$41,700	($10,000)	$7,000	$4,000	$8,700	($12,000)
SUM [5.1Yr - 10Yr]	($11,000)	$53,000	($15,000)	($12,000)	$0	$21,000	($5,000)
SUM [10.1Yr - 30Yr]	$40,000	$40,000	$5,000	$0	$0	$35,000	$0
Outrite bpv	$22,700	$208,700	$0	$5,000	$9,000	$29,700	($21,000)
Swap vs Futures	($10,000)	$110,000	$50,000	($5,000)	($55,000)		
Swap vs Bonds	($30,000)	$80,000	$25,000			($55,000)	
Option Risk							
7 Day Carry+Theta	($2,000)		$120,000	$0	($7,000)	($55,000)	($60,000)
Vega (1%)	$95,000	$695,000	($300,000)		$45,000	$150,000	$200,000
Gamma (10bp)	$22,000		($70,000)		$10,000	$32,000	$50,000
Portfolio Leverage	6.74	16.14					

FIGURE 8.1   Sample risk report of interest rate risk in a portfolio.

- 7 Day Carry+Theta section captures how the portfolio decays in terms of profit and loss. Assuming nothing in the market changes for seven days, this section will capture what the profit and loss of the portfolio would be just from a decay of the positions. This risk arises from options time decay as well as the roll down of interest rate positions down the yield curve.
- Vega (1%) captures the risk in the portfolio from a change in volatility levels. The Absolute SUM field of the vega exposure adds the positive and negative vega exposures because theoretically the volatility on the long vega exposures could decline while the volatility on the short vega exposures could rise, thereby increasing the risk of a long and a short position, instead of reducing it.
- Gamma (10bp) captures the changes in the delta risk of the portfolio as the interest rates move up by ten basis points. Gamma is called the second-order effect on a portfolio as it changes the delta risk of a portfolio if interest rates move by a large amount.
- Portfolio Leverage is the calculation of the net delta exposure as a ratio of the assets under management. In an interest rate derivatives portfolio, all the delta exposure across the maturities is converted to a 10-year equivalent instrument for addition purposes. The option notionals are taken at their current delta. We further assume that the fund size is $100 million for the leverage calculation. 6.74 leverage assumes full correlation benefits across the deltas of different countries, while 16.14 assumes no correlation benefits at all.

The abovementioned risk parameters give a pretty well-rounded picture of the portfolio that a hedge fund manager should not have a problem divulging. It contains no position level information and thus will not reveal the exact source of alpha or the intended price points and holding period.

To the untrained eye the above risk report would not raise questions, but there are six circled red flags that should jump out to any trader who has traded these strategies in these stated markets.

1. **Correlation Risk:** The total delta risk in the portfolio is very small while the sum of the absolute risk is quite large. This shows a lot of spread risk between the various interest rate buckets as well as between countries. This should prompt questions about the spread risks and thereby the hedge fund manager's views on them that the fund of funds investment panel should be aware of.
2. **Basis Risk:** The portfolio is carrying two large swaps versus futures basis positions, the first in the United States and the second in New Zealand. There is a potential liquidity problem with the New Zealand

basis position. Anybody who has traded the New Zealand interest rate futures market would know that it is extremely difficult to source liquidity in New Zealand bond futures, therefore a position size equivalent to NZD 260 million worth of five-year bonds would be a very illiquid position and worthy of ongoing due diligence.

3. **KRW Bonds:** The risk report shows a position in swaps versus bonds in South Korea. South Korean Won is a non-deliverable currency, and the government bond market is closed to outside investors. South Korea and several other Asian countries adopted such measures to protect their currencies and asset markets from foreign speculators after the 1998 Asian crisis. Therefore, an investor has to have a local balance sheet to be able to purchase Korean government bonds. The other way around it is by borrowing a local bank's balance sheet and getting the exposure through a derivative instrument called a Total Return Swap where all cash flows are net settled in U.S. dollars. Most likely the hedge fund manager has established this position through a total return swap, in which case he is exposed to other risk factors such as government regulations, bank's balance sheet restrictions, currency fixing risk, and a nonfungible product, risks that are typical of an emerging market investment.

4. **Large Vega Exposure:** The risk report shows a relatively small outright vega risk, but the vega spread risk between countries is almost six times larger than the sum of the vega risks. This should once again prompt questions of the hedge fund manager regarding his market views.

5. **Large Short Option Position in United States:** The negative vega and gamma point to a very large short option position in the United States, which overall seems to be balanced out by long options in other countries. This is a large spread position that could be negatively impacted by big interest rate moves in the United States that are not offset in countries with offsetting long gamma positions.

6. **Portfolio Leverage of a Derivatives Portfolio:** In the risk report we see the leverage numbers, which take into account only the delta exposures of the instruments. A derivatives-based portfolio could carry very little delta exposure yet have a lot of risk in the portfolio arising from the option positions. An uncorrelated vega exposure of \$695,000 could result in large positive or negative returns if the option implied volatilities were to change dramatically. Similarly, a large gamma exposure could also change the position deltas, resulting in big positive or negative returns. Therefore, while looking at the portfolio leverage levels, it is important to look at not just the delta leverage but also the size of the vega and gamma exposures.

Hypothetical FX (Foreign Exchange) Risk Report

Figure 8.2 is a sample risk report of the currency risk in a portfolio. The first section captures the linear or the delta risk in the portfolio. The numbers represent the currency notionals in each country.

■ The report is broken out by the various countries that the fund trades in, i.e., United States, Australia, New Zealand, South Korea, and Hong Kong.
■ A positive number indicates a long position in the currency of that country, and a negative number represents a short position in the currency of that country.
■ All the numbers for other countries are converted into U.S. dollars for ease of comparison.
■ Portfolio SUM is the addition of all the risk numbers, positive and negative.
■ Absolute SUM is the addition of all the absolute risks, assuming no correlation benefits.
■ FX Cash Balance is the actual cash balance in each country that needs to be funded.

The second section illustrates the second-order risk in the currency options portfolio.

■ 7 Day Carry+Theta section captures how the portfolio decays in terms of profit and loss. Assuming nothing in the market changes for seven days, this section will capture what the profit and loss of the portfolio would be just from a decay of the positions. This risk arises from options time decay as well as the funding cost of the currencies in their local interest rates.

			FX RISK				
Delta Risk	Portfolio SUM	Absolute SUM	USD	AUD	NZD	KRW	HKD
Notional	$225,000,000		($225,000,000)	$45,000,000	($45,000,000)	($180,000,000)	$65,000,000
FX Cash Balance	($250,000,000)		$250,000,000	$45,000,000	($45,000,000)	$100,000,000	($350,000,000)
Option Risk							
7 Day Carry+Theta	$118,000		$120,000	$0	($7,000)	($55,000)	$60,000
Vega (1%)	($305,000)	$695,000	($300,000)		$45,000	$150,000	($200,000)
Gamma (0.25%)	($78,000)		($70,000)		$10,000	$32,000	($50,000)
Portfolio Leverage	2.25						

FIGURE 8.2 Sample risk report of currency risk in a portfolio.

- Vega (1%) captures the risk in the portfolio from a change in volatility levels.
- Gamma (0.25%) captures the changes in the delta risk of the portfolio as the currency levels move up by 0.25 percent. Gamma is called the second-order effect on a portfolio because it changes the delta risk of a portfolio if currency levels move by a large amount.
- Portfolio Leverage is the calculation of the net delta exposure on the FX portfolio as a ratio of the assets under management. The option notionals are taken at their current delta. We further assume that the fund size is $100 million for the leverage calculation. As currency exposure requires a long position in one country and the same amount of a short position in another country, we only need a portfolio SUM leverage number of 2.25.

As in the interest rate section, there are several red flags in this sample FX risk report as well, which are outlined here:

1. **FX Cash Balance in KRW:** A positive cash balance in Korean Won means that the portfolio has an onshore balance sheet in South Korea. As described above, South Korean markets are closed to outside investors and only onshore registered counterparties are allowed to hold Korean Won currency and assets. An onshore balance sheet in a country with capital controls poses some liquidity and capital access risks. The fund manager's ability to withdraw capital out of the country could be limited by government restrictions, which can change at any time. Furthermore, in an effort to stem outflow of capital, the government might impose currency non-convertibility restrictions, which would imply that the Korean Won held by the fund would not be convertible into any other currency.

2. **FX Cash Balance in HKD:** The fund is carrying a large short position in Hong Kong Dollars that it is most likely funded overnight or on a short-term basis. A lot of traders will run a funding basis position—i.e., long cash in a country with high interest rates and short cash in the country with low interest rates. They take a risk on the funding rate differential itself. This risk can be quite substantial depending on the market environment. I was trading the Asian currency funding book in Hong Kong in 1997 when speculative attacks to devalue Asian currencies were in full swing. On October 22, 1997, the Hong Kong Monetary Authority, in an effort to protect the HKD, decided to restrict the funding of short HKD positions, thereby sending the overnight funding rate on short HKD borrowings to 1000 percent. Funding a short $350 million position for one day would have resulted in a loss of

$9.6 million ($350 million × 1,000%/365). When you live through days like these in the markets and survive, they leave a very deep and lasting impact on your memory. Therefore, I am always very skeptical of large short cash funding positions in emerging markets that could be exposed to massive and sudden interest rate moves.

3. **Option exposure in HKD:** The vega and gamma profile of the HKD bucket is implying a short option position in HKD. HKD, as mentioned earlier, is pegged to the USD, i.e., the USD/HKD exchange rate for all intents and purposes is fixed around 7.8000. Therefore, currency volatility levels are very low, around 1 percent. Selling this cheap volatility as a carry trade is not a prudent way to generate returns. But, from time to time speculative attacks will cause the volatilities and currency forwards to move to attractive levels where a positive carry position in anticipation of the currency peg staying would make sense. The fund of funds investment panel would have to make the decision whether the carry position established by the hedge fund manager is prudent given the market levels or not.

4. **Large Vega Exposure:** Just as in the interest rate risk report, the FX risk report shows a relatively small outright vega risk but the vega spread risk between countries is almost six times larger than the sum of the vega risks.

With the above-described sample risk reports, hopefully I have shown that to conduct appropriate strategy-level ongoing due diligence on the hedge fund investment, the funds of funds need trading expertise, market experience, as well as necessary risk management and derivative securities knowledge. Furthermore, the funds of funds need to stay on top of not just the macroeconomic developments in the market to assess beta versus alpha opportunities, but also individual market developments to assess the idiosyncratic risks that might be developing in those markets. The current fund of funds investment panels are far from adept at grasping these concepts, but a fund of funds investment panel that is run like a Wall Street proprietary trading desk will have the capabilities to do just that.

MANAGER STOP LOSS AND LINKED REDEMPTIONS

When a hedge fund manager goes through the initial due diligence process with a fund of funds, he is skeptical and unsure of how much capital he will receive and when it would be invested. Due diligence is not an exact science and a lot of factors go into the decision-making process. Often the hedge fund manager is surprised by the investor's decision or the amount of capital invested. While the investment process can sometimes be subjective, I would claim that the redemption process should never come as a surprise to either the hedge fund manager or to the investor. The hedge fund manager should know when he has hit his stop loss with a particular investor, and an investor should know that he will get his entire capital back at the specified time without having to climb over any gates.

Before I proceed further, I want to explain what a redemption gate is and state that it is a very egregious concept. When a hedge fund faces redemptions in excess of a pre-stated percentage of the fund's capital, this ranging between 10 and 25 percent usually, the hedge fund manager can at his own discretion restrict the amount of capital being redeemed. Hedge fund managers will argue that it serves to protect the interests of the other investors in the fund; I would argue that it serves to protect the financial interests of the hedge fund manager. The concept of redemption gates comes as a part of the entitlement package of moving to the hedge fund industry and needs to be abolished. A hedge fund manager will justify the gate by claiming that trying to close out a significant portion of the portfolio would materially affect the price received and thereby hurt the fund's performance. The typical time between a redemption request and the actual redemption is anywhere from one to six months. This notice period is defined by the hedge fund manager based on his calculations of the hedge fund size and the underlying market liquidity. If a fund manager cannot liquidate his entire portfolio within this stated time, then he has:

- Grown his fund to an unmanageable size, or
- Not sized his positions based on market liquidity. As explained earlier, position sizing based on market liquidity is a dynamic process and not a static one.

Either way, the manager has breached risk management principles. Therefore, by instituting a redemption gate, the manager is either claiming that he intends to breach his risk management principles or that he is simply protecting his financial interests. I would place my bets on the latter.

When a trader is hired on a proprietary trading desk of a Wall Street bank, he is given a trading mandate, defined risk capital, a defined payoff formula for compensation, and a defined stop loss level. The stop loss level defines in no uncertain terms the maximum drawdown the trader is allowed from peak to trough as well as on an annual basis before he will be shut down, which means fired. The peak to trough concept is illustrated in Table 8.2.

Hypothetical Returns of a Proprietary Trader

Peak to Trough

TABLE 8.2   Peak to Trough

Month	Monthly Returns	Cumulative Returns
January	1.00%	1.00%
February	1.40%	2.40%
March	1.30%	3.70%
April	1.30%	5.00%
May	1.50%	6.50%
June	−0.80%	5.70%
July	−1.40%	4.30%
August	−0.80%	3.50%
September	1.50%	5.00%
October	1.00%	6.00%
November	1.00%	7.00%
December	1.00%	8.00%

Chart of Cumulative Returns   Figure 8.3 shows the hypothetical cumulative returns of a proprietary trader. This trader lost money in the months of June, July, and August such that his cumulative returns fell from point A, the peak, to point B, the trough, for a total amount of 3 percent of capital. If the trader's peak to trough drawdown limit had been smaller than 3 percent, then he would have been stopped out and his positions closed down. This is down to ensure that one or two bad positions do not undo the profitability of the rest of the portfolio and helps in preserving the portfolio's profits. Also, the peak to trough is a function of the accumulated profits up to that point. Higher the amassed profits, higher the peak to trough drawdown limits and vice versa. Similarly, the trader is also assigned an annual drawdown limit. A young trader with no track record will be generally on a very tight leash and assigned a relatively small drawdown. As he amasses profits, his annual drawdown limits also increase.

The drawdown limits described above are a function of the strategy deployed as well. A strategy could be a high-volatility strategy because of a combination of the markets it is deployed in, the instruments used to express it, as well as the principle behind it. For a high-volatility strategy,

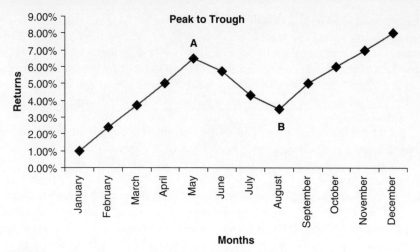

FIGURE 8.3 Hypothetical cumulative returns of a proprietary trader.

the drawdown limits will be higher because the expected returns will also be commensurately higher and vice versa.

These drawdown limits enforce risk management discipline on the trader so that he can manage his position sizing and stop loss limits accordingly. No trader wants to end his trading career because of one or two bad trades, so he will break down the position size as a function of the risk capital assigned to him, the drawdown limits, and the stop loss tolerances. The trader's interests and the employer's interests get aligned as the trader starts to take ownership of the portfolio risk management himself. In this scenario, a trader will lose his capital base and eventually his job not because of making one or even a string of bad calls. He will lose his job if either he does not follow his own risk management principles, a weakness of character, or if he repeatedly makes several bad calls, in which case he never had the acumen for being a trader in the first place. Either way the decision never comes as a surprise to the trader.

Once this trader moves to the world of hedge fund trading, this drawdown oversight is lost. The hedge fund manager feels a certain amount of entitlement that he is not beholden to predefined drawdown limits anymore. The fund of funds CIO has no expertise in the field of trading, so he does not know how to evaluate the volatility of a particular strategy and therefore assign drawdown limits, so he rarely stipulates these in his investment. The expectations of the fund of funds versus that of the hedge fund manager are not aligned, so when a drawdown occurs, the fund of funds investor panics and does not know what to expect in the coming months, while the hedge fund manager does not have a guideline to base his position sizing and stop losses on. The fund of funds then bases its capital redemption decisions on panic rather than on an educated response, which upsets the hedge fund managers in return because they feel that their drawdown expectations were not understood by the fund of funds. This is one of the main reasons why the funds of funds are not welcome investors by the hedge fund community.

The drawdown limits need to be determined by the funds of funds based on the risk management guidelines of the fund. The fund of funds needs to assign both peak to trough as well as annual drawdown limits on its capital. Once these limits have been negotiated with the hedge fund manager, side letters need to be negotiated to ensure that the fund of funds would be able to redeem its capital as soon as these limits are breached without penalty and delay. These drawdown limits would be based on the hedge fund manager's own stated risk management guidelines. Therefore, if the risk management guidelines are breached, it would imply a lack of infrastructure or worse, lack of discipline. In either case, the fund of funds needs to exercise its risk management discipline and redeem its investment. A well-defined hedge fund stop loss methodology will make sure that there are no surprises for either the hedge fund manager or the fund of funds investor.

NOT 10 PERCENT, MAJORITY EVERY TIME

Some critics of my described fund of funds model will say that the hedge funds do not offer the transparency, desired liquidity, or description of the strategy to implement the stated model. First, the number of such funds was a select group to start with as most hedge funds do offer monthly liquidity and daily risk reporting. Additionally, after the recent market rout and a spate of frauds, a lot more hedge funds will be more than willing to increase transparency.

I want to briefly digress and talk about one of my favorite TV shows on BBC America, called *Dragon's Den*. I would highly recommend that people watch this show to see how a group of five multimillionaire venture capitalists perform due diligence on new business ideas and negotiate an investment. These venture capitalists have hands-on experience in various industries across the board. In a relatively short period of time, they are presented with business ideas, and they ask very probing questions on the product, patents, marketing, and financial valuations of the company. These questions do not come off any preprinted questionnaire. Once these investors realize that the new invention or business idea is viable, they provide not only the funding but also their expertise and in return ask for a large stake in the business. The larger the stake, the more control they have over the destiny of their own investments.

I wanted to mention *Dragon's Den* to draw a comparison to the fund of funds model that places an investment cap of 10 to 20 percent of the total assets under management of a hedge fund. As I have discussed in my earlier chapters, the only benefit this provides is a sense of "safety in numbers," which arises from an insecurity the fund of funds has in its own due diligence process. Under the new prescribed fund of funds model where traders are running investment divisions of fund of funds, the conviction in the due diligence should increase. If the fund of funds decides to invest in a new hedge fund manager, it should provide a sizable investment, irrespective of how many other investors are invested alongside. Mind you, I am not suggesting that the fund of funds put all its capital into a handful of funds. A fund of funds still needs to be diversified into several underlying hedge funds, but it should not shy away from becoming as large an investor in a hedge fund manager as possible to gain leverage in negotiations. In return, the chances are that the fund of funds will be able to receive complete transparency, capacity, stop loss limits, and perhaps even fee reductions. The hedge fund manager would also stand to benefit from the experience of the fund of fund's investment panel. At the end of the day, every legitimate hedge fund wants an educated and rational investor. If the hedge funds do not offer the requisite transparency or liquidity, I would suggest that the fund of funds move on to a hedge fund that does. If you did not know the color or make of a car, would you buy it? Then why would you invest billions in a strategy that you do not understand or that you have no information on either?

A lack of conviction in due diligence processes and mishaps along the way has made it extremely difficult for the young aspiring and talented hedge fund manager to get funded. Investors have adopted a safety in numbers approach and rushed to the gates of the few large hedge funds, making them even larger and often less compliant to the investors' wishes. Therefore, it is most likely that it will be some of these large hedge funds that will balk at the idea of stop loss limits and requisite transparency. The recent financial crisis has proven that some of these so-called mavens of the industry have fared no better and actually much worse than the smaller and nimbler hedge funds. In fact, the larger institutions are more likely to exhibit style drift, become mired in illiquid positions, and thereby put up gates and lock up capital when an investor wants his money back.

Perhaps my prescribed fund of funds model will return a sense of entrepreneurialism and accountability to the hedge fund industry as the smaller players get the requisite funding. In return, the investor community will get more transparency and thereby more control over their investment.

ONGOING DUE DILIGENCE: IT IS NOT JUST ABOUT RETURNS

As long as a hedge fund manager keeps posting positive returns, he will be left alone by the fund of funds investors. Most likely he will keep getting new capital inflows with little more than a cursory visit to the offices, so some more boxes can be checked on preprinted documents. As soon as the hedge fund manager enters a drawdown period, the questions start arising. If the drawdown is severe, a sense of panic starts to ensue and redemption notices start piling up. But as soon as the very same manager starts to perform well again, all is forgiven, and the same fund of funds starts lining up at the door to reinvest. Buying high and selling low is the mantra of the panic-struck investor. This is no way to conduct ongoing due diligence on a hedge fund investment. Returns are the result of a process, the due diligence should be performed on the process to make sure that the process is functioning as it should. If the process starts to break down, the investor should redeem his investment, and if the process is sound, the investor should stay committed, irrespective of the returns. A caveat to this statement is that the stop loss limits are not breached, as stop loss limits are an integral part of that process.

Funds of funds provide the capital and pay the hedge fund manager fees. From a commercial standpoint, the funds of funds are the bosses, and the fund manager works for them. The funds of funds need to realize this and start acting like it. Ongoing due diligence should involve the following steps in terms of importance and a top-down approach:

1. The original five inviolable commandments, mentioned at the start of the chapter, are still in place that ensure the required transparency and veracity of the information coming out of a hedge fund.
2. Stated position, monthly, annual, and peak to trough drawdown limits are being followed.
3. The professional trading staff with the core competencies is still intact.
4. Risk reports need to be monitored on at least a weekly basis and any red flags, as shown earlier in the chapter from the hypothetical reports, need to be addressed with the fund manager.
5. Monthly telephone calls are made to go over the profit and loss attributions, market views, and positioning opportunities going forward.
6. The monthly telephone calls should be substituted with onsite visits every second or third month for face-to-face discussions. This opportunity should be used for discussions with some of the other trading staff as well to gauge the firm's morale and other information about the company that would not be apparent in a telephone call. This visit should also be used to pick one or two of the recent winning and losing trades to dig deeply

into what went right and what went wrong and, more important, why. Because the new fund of funds model will have a panel of experienced traders, they can also offer insight to the fund manager.

7. Keep the relationship professional; avoid due diligence over a game of golf or dinner and drinks. Sometimes the fund manager might become more relaxed in a setting outside the office, in which case let the fund manager do the drinking rather than the other way around.

CHAPTER 9

Correct Risk Due Diligence

What has completely baffled me about the fund of funds industry is that it is always clamoring for increased transparency. It certainly is a very pertinent request, and it also makes for good newspaper headlines and aids in marketing for the fund of funds. But the question is, What does the fund of funds industry do with this transparency? It certainly does not have the qualified personnel to monitor the risk reports provided by the hedge funds. Most large and small hedge funds these days provide regular risk reports to their investors. Some funds even provide daily risk reporting through a website access. If the fund of funds industry was actually doing its job and monitoring these risk reports, then how could it let some of the largest hedge funds lose upwards of 40 percent in 2008? When hedge funds that market themselves as low volatility safe funds can lose as much as 30 percent in a single month, as quite a few relative value funds did in October 2008, then clearly risk limits must have been breached.

These risks should have been quite evident in the risk reports provided to the fund of funds industry. Did the funds of funds understand these risk reports? Did they bother to even look at them and ask the right questions? It was their fiduciary duty to do so, as the investors entrusted them with their capital and paid them fees to perform those tasks. The bottom line is that all the transparency in the world will not mean much if the fund of funds investor does not have the skills required to decipher it.

I have listed some of the typical risk management questions that a fund of funds analyst will ask from his preprinted AIMA questionnaire. Some of these questions are not pertinent, and to an untrained eye some of the answers to these questions might fail to shed light on the true risk in a portfolio.

POSITION CONCENTRATION, SO WHAT?

A typical response from a hedge fund manager could look like this: We diversify our portfolio across countries, industries, and strategies to ensure that there is no concentration of risk. We further undertake stress tests to minimize correlation among different parts of the portfolio. Some hedge funds might even provide guidelines to the maximum amount of risk any particular sector might be assigned. These guidelines in marketing pitch books do not mean much as they are often overwritten by the Offering Memorandum, which usually gives the hedge fund manager carte blanche. I remember a hedge fund manager, an acquaintance of mine, who once boasted, "I can take your capital and go to Vegas and you can't do a damn thing about it." He must have had good lawyers drafting his Offering Memorandum.

Every fund of funds wants to hear that the hedge fund manager will not put all his eggs in one basket and that he will not be concentrated in any one country, industry, or strategy. This question actually has very little relevance, as I have shown earlier that given the strong linkages between the global economies and asset classes, diversification by asset class and geography does not work. As an example, a hedge fund manager might have positions in the United States and Asia that benefit from a rate cut scenario, and he might be long U.S. dollars versus the EUR. He might have established his interest rate strategy in the United States through interest rate derivatives and in Asia through currency forwards. Based on the fund of fund's risk methodology, the hedge fund manager would be diversified because he was not concentrated in any one country, asset class, or strategy. Furthermore, in normal functioning markets the correlation between the three positions would also be very low. But a closer look at the risk would show that all the three strategies would move in tandem in the case of a global economic slowdown, as it happened in 2008. Some funds of funds will require that the hedge fund manager run a scenario analysis on his portfolio to mimic the market crisis of 1998 (Asia) or 2000 (Internet) or 2003 (U.S. deflation risk scenario). Now even 2008 (credit crisis) will be added to that list. The problem with this scenario analysis is that each of those periods was different in both cause and effect from the others; therefore, a scenario analysis of a particular period has very little bearing on how the portfolio might perform in the next market crisis.

The second problem with this question is that it unnecessarily hampers the hedge fund manager from generating alpha. Some of the largest profitable trades in the history of hedge funds have been made on single concentrated bets, e.g., George Soros's bet against the Pound Sterling in 1992, the Asian crisis of 1998, the Internet boom and then the bust of the late 1990s, the Asian equity boom of 2004–2007, and last but not the least John Paulson's $20 billion profit by betting on the credit market meltdown of 2008. Position concentration can cut both ways. Amaranth Advisors lost 65 percent of its fund on a single natural gas trade. Therefore, the relevance of the position concentration question is nebulous at best. The real question is not position concentration but how that position is managed from a stop loss basis and market liquidity basis.

The hedge fund manager should be left to produce alpha, whether it is through a handful of positions or through many. It is the fund of funds' responsibility to create a diversified portfolio and not the hedge fund manager's. To draw an analogy with the mutual fund industry, a mutual fund manager who bought Google in 2004 would have been very happy with his pick, even though Google has always been a "one trick pony," specializing as a search engine. Most successful traders on Wall Street proprietary desks specialize in one or two strategies in one or two markets as well. If the fund of funds manager understands how his hedge funds are positioned, then he can create his own diversification by investing in managers that have different exposures. Diversification is one of the reasons why investors invest in funds of funds and not into hedge funds directly.

MANAGEMENT OF STOP LOSS LIMITS: THE BE-ALL AND END-ALL

Stop loss limits and their management are the core piece of any risk management methodology. Everything else is secondary and works in conjunction with stop losses. If a trader is right more than 60 percent of the time, he is considered a good trader, but his level of profitability is determined by his ability to apply his stop loss discipline on the 40 percent of the losing trades. Nearly every hedge fund manager will have the most rational and well-thought-out stop loss plan and will profess to apply it diligently 100 percent of the time. If that were the case, you would not see hedge funds amassing the type of losses they did in 2008 or cases like Amaranth Advisors or Long Term Capital Management.

The application of stop loss limits and their management has to occur at a tiered level starting at the position level, rising up to the trader level, and finally at the portfolio level. Once a position reaches a predefined price target, it needs to be closed out. Once a trader reaches a predefined loss threshold, he needs to be shut down, and when the portfolio reaches a certain monthly or annual loss, the portfolio needs to be shut down as well, at least for a period of time. A hedge fund manager needs to let his investors know what these tiered stop loss levels are, and the investor needs to ensure that they are being followed diligently, month after month, year after year. Following the stop loss limits is at a hedge fund manager's discretion, but monitoring these stop loss limits is the fund of funds' fiduciary responsibility. Once a well-defined risk management methodology fails, the investor needs to realize that the fault lay not with the methodology but with the discipline of the hedge fund manager. As mentioned before, trading discipline is strongly linked to the character of a person, and if it fails once, it will most likely fail again.

There are several pitfalls that can even derail the best-laid risk management plans. Stop losses have to take into account market liquidity, bid-offer spreads, gap risk, and position sizing as well as loss of anonymity. In normal functioning markets, liquidity is ample, bid-offer spreads are tight, and gap risk is low enough that a trader can get away with large position sizes. But when the markets freeze up, even a well-thought-out stop loss management system will fail due to lack of liquidity or wide bid-offer spreads. Monitoring these key parameters has to be a dynamic process that is conducted on at least a weekly basis. Position sizing has to be constantly modified as a function of changing market conditions to maintain the effectiveness of the stop loss system.

Gap risk is a binary risk for which no stop loss system is possible. If a trader takes a position on a binary outcome that will be "Yes" or "No," he is exposing himself to the rewards as well as the risks of that outcome. Examples of gap risk can be found every time a company announces earnings or big macroeconomic data is released. If the announced data is far from the market consensus, the market adjusts to incorporate the news almost instantaneously with little or no traded volume. Another example of gap risk is when lack of reliable data causes the market to panic. When very little information is available for the market to find an equilibrium level, the market will use any traded volume as information and gap violently on very low traded volumes. Another example of gap risk is around changes in government policies, for example, the breakdown of currency pegs like the breaking of the Chinese peg on July 21, 2005. These market gaps can be as small as a tenth of a percent to as large as 10 percent or greater, but in every case they are generally a very large multiple of the normal bid-offer spread. The hedge fund investor needs to realize the gap risks in a hedge fund's portfolio so he is not surprised, either positively or negatively, when that move occurs.

Loss of anonymity is as dangerous a risk as any and can foil the best-laid stop loss plans. In 2000 when I was trading a proprietary book at BNP Paribas in Singapore, I had amassed a very large position in 5-year versus 10-year Hong Kong Dollar swap spreads. This position was executed through the OTC (over-the-counter) or live broker market, and I did not have the anonymity benefits of a futures exchange. This position was easily a month's worth of normal market liquidity, and after a while it seemed like the entire market knew about it. So every time the market moved in my favor and I tried to get a price to unwind the position, the market would move the price away. I remember one day the Hong Kong Dollar swap curve flattened, with the first price of the day marking the 5-year–10-year spread flatter by 10bps. As I entered the market to start unwinding my position, the market started moving the prices against me. I traded twice in market standard sizes, and the next price on the 5-year–10-year spread was quoted at unchanged levels from the previous day. Usually, for the market to move 10 basis points in the 5-year–10-year spread would require twenty to 25 times the size that I actually traded. This created an absurd shape in the yield curve, but the market was out to squeeze me out of my position. I had to lie low for almost six months and engage in guerilla warfare before I was able to ever get out of my position. I swore after that incident never to amass a position so large that I would lose the benefits of anonymity and jeopardize my risk management.

Finally, I want to touch on the subject of doubling up on losing positions. At the onset of a trade, every seasoned trader will define a trading stop loss or will construct his position such that it has a structural stop loss associated with it. When that price point is triggered, the trader will close out his position and live to fight another day. But sometimes a trader will make the decision to double up on a losing position and justify his decision as, "Well, if I liked it at twenty five, I should love it at twenty" or "I am lowering my average entry cost in to this position by doubling up." There is nothing wrong with either of these arguments, as long as they were made before the position was initiated and therefore sized appropriately. A trader might like a trade very much, but he may be unsure of the best entry point. In this case he might decide to enter into half or even a third of the position and wait for a lower price point to increase the size of the position. In this case, he is adding to a losing trade, but it was a part of his strategy at the onset. When a trader enters into his position on day one in full size and then tries to justify adding to a losing position after it has gone through his stop loss target, then he is trading based on emotions and ego, not to a plan. That is a recipe for disaster.

OVER-LEVERAGE AND ILLIQUIDITY

In my experience, more good risk-abiding traders have been hurt by over-leverage than any other single factor. And second, in most of those times a lack of market liquidity has played a big part in it; therefore, I am putting leverage and liquidity together as a single linked risk parameter.

Leverage in a portfolio should be a function of the strategy, the underlying liquidity of the market, and the instruments used in expressing that strategy. A long-short strategy that is generally expressed by buying the underlying stocks or bonds utilizes low leverage, while a relative value or arbitrage strategy that is trying to capture small gains needs to be magnified by employing high leverage.

Leverage ratios are a relative concept and an absolute number like five to one or 25 to 1 is quite meaningless. Yet, most funds of funds will feel a lot more comfortable if they are able to check the box that says five to one in their preprinted questionnaire rather than the one that says 25 to 1. The reason why leverage is a relative concept is because it depends upon the underlying market's liquidity and the way that leverage has been deployed.

Market Liquidity

A size of a position should be a function of the underlying market's liquidity. If a market trades 100 lots in a normal day, and the total position size is 500 lots, then the trader loses the ability to maneuver as well as loses benefits of anonymity as the market sooner or later always finds out the owners of the largest positions. If the position starts to go wrong, it can create a feeding frenzy because the market would keep driving the prices against the big position holders trying to liquidate in an illiquid market. In scenarios like this, the daily market liquidity would fall from 100 lots to more like twenty lots a day.

Borrowed Cash

A position can be leveraged by borrowing cash from a prime broker to buy stocks or bonds or by establishing a position through derivative instruments on margin. Derivative instruments' margin requirements are very small and can provide massive leverage, sometimes as high as 100 to 1 on swap agreements. A lot of relative value and arbitrage funds that are trying to capture small price discrepancies usually will establish their positions through derivative instruments and utilize leverage around fifteen to twenty times the capital. Leverage is defined as:

$$\text{Portfolio Leverage} = \frac{\text{Position Size}}{\text{Fund's Assets Under Management}}$$

Say a fund starts out with a leverage ratio of 15 to 1 in his portfolio. Assume that the positions in his portfolio decline by 2 percent in value, but due to wrong positioning and market illiquidity, he cannot reduce his position size. The mark to market on his portfolio will give him a loss of 30 percent (15 × 2%). A reduction in the denominator in the above equation automatically increases the leverage of the portfolio, even though the manager may not have placed any new trades at all. A 30 percent decrease in the assets under management will increase the portfolio leverage from 15 to 1 to 21.4 to 1. This vicious cycle would not have to continue very long before the fund would be officially defunct.

The other risk to borrowed cash is that the margin requirements can be changed by the lender if the lender senses potential credit risk on part of the borrower. In this case, the borrower could be forced to liquidate his positions to meet the increased margin requirements, which can result in losses for the portfolio.

Long Gamma Leverage

Leverage is a vital part of a lot of different strategies, and the key is in how this leverage has been established. The safest way to establish the leverage is through a long gamma method, or simply put, by buying options.

Say, a $100 million fund buys 20 delta options on a notional of $1.5 billion.

On a delta basis, which is the correct way to measure the leverage of a derivatives portfolio, the portfolio leverage would be 3:

$$\frac{\$1.5 \text{ billion} \times 20\%}{\$100 \text{ million}}$$

If the portfolio manager's view was incorrect and the market went against him, the option deltas would go to zero and his leverage as well will go to zero.

If the portfolio manager's view was correct and the market moved in his direction, then the option deltas would go to 100 percent and the portfolio leverage would rise to 15.

$$\frac{\$1.5 \text{ billion} \times 100\%}{\$100 \text{ million}}$$

Therefore, the portfolio leverage rises only when the positions are in the money and falls as the positions go out of the money, which is a very safe way to deploy leverage. There is some risk to this as well, because the market liquidity could dry up as the positions go in the money, and the trader has a difficult time locking in the gains. But in a long gamma scenario, the trader has a few things going for him even in an illiquid market.

1. If the options expire, he gets to lock in the gains.
2. He has the choice of locking in gains by either selling the options or delta hedging.
3. He would most likely find the necessary liquidity because his winning position will be the one providing the market with the liquidity that the market needs. If everybody is clamoring for apples and you are the only one holding apples, you will most likely not just get to sell all your apples but also define the price at which you sell them.

Therefore, defining a hard number on leverage is quite meaningless. The hedge fund investor needs to understand the leverage as a function of the strategy, market's underlying liquidity, and, more important, how that leverage is established and how it will behave in a stressful market environment.

HEDGING: WILL THE MARKET LET YOU SHORT?

There is an entire section in the AIMA risk management questionnaire that addresses questions on portfolio hedging. So there is no surprise that the fund of funds analyst will regurgitate the same questions diligently and jot down the answers in his preprinted sheets. The questions range from position sizing to frequency of hedging to managing short positions and whether short positions are meant to generate profits as well. When I was asked these questions, I was bemused, as I am sure several other hedge fund managers have been as well. The reason for my amusement was because these questions are completely nonsensical. Frequency of hedging is not a defined parameter; a trader does not set himself a target to hedge every day or every 1 percent price move. If a trader has strong conviction in the move in a stock price, he will stay with the trend for days or even weeks and for 5 percent, 10 percent, or even larger moves. He will hedge only when his conviction starts to wane or he hits his stop loss. Therefore, trying to define a number for hedging frequency of an entire portfolio is impossible. So most likely a hedge fund manager chuckles at the naivety of the investor and puts down what he feels the fund of funds investor want to hear, which is "on a very regular basis."

The most important question that should be asked is whether instruments are available for hedging or going short in a particular market and the cost associated with them. If a market does not allow the trader to go short, then the trader is employing a long-only strategy. Any market that has well-developed liquidity in derivatives instruments, whether exchange traded or OTC, will provide means of going long or short and therefore hedging a portfolio. Asian markets do not offer any substantive means of shorting stocks or bonds, yet fund of funds have filled out reams of due diligence questionnaires and funded a bunch of beta strategies disguised as alpha strategies since 2004. I can only wonder what was fed to them in terms of answers to the hedging questions and how much if any was actually understood.

A lot of long-short strategies will profess to run a market-neutral portfolio on the basis of hedging their long holdings with other correlated short holdings. The key to their hedging principle here is correlation. Often these correlations are calculated by crunching historical data. Correlations are not a constant and often break down due to idiosyncratic risk. For example, a long Google versus a short Yahoo position is not a hedged market-neutral position: It runs two distinct idiosyncratic risk positions. The trade is exposed to both Google and Yahoo company news, even though both stocks might fall or rise in tandem on a normal day with the general market.

Another important hedging principle to understand is that the best hedge for any security is that very security itself. A position established by using options such that the maximum loss is defined upfront and is the premium paid on that position is a perfectly hedged position. Any other hedge, whether it is a position offset by a correlated short position or a hedge managed by a stop loss scheme, is at best an imperfect hedge.

The fund of funds should make sure that means of shorting a market exist, because that will ensure that their investment is in an alpha strategy and not a disguised beta strategy. Beyond this, any further questions on hedging are really meaningless, and more attention should be paid to stop loss methodology and regular monitoring to ensure its strict adherence on a regular basis.

CHAPTER 10

Interviewing a Hedge Fund Manager

Interviewing a hedge fund manager should not be about running through a list of questions in some prescribed document by an inexperienced analyst, but about thoughtful probing of the manager's experience, market understanding, risk-taking ability, and above all, strength of character. First as a bookrunner and then as a proprietary trader, I have gone through several rounds of interviews with senior trading managers from Wall Street banks. As a hedge fund manager, I have conducted more than 200 meetings with funds of funds and other investors as well. I would say that most of the questions that are asked can be found in one of the several books written on the industry, and the answers to these questions prove of little or no value. But there are some questions that are truly probing and can shed light on a trader's intelligence, expertise, and character. Proper due diligence of a hedge fund manager is the fiduciary responsibility of every fund of funds, pension fund, endowment, and family office that has been trusted with an investor's assets. It can be the difference between investing in a safe, alpha-producing vehicle and losing the entire investment to the next Bernie Madoff.

RELATIONSHIP

An investment in a hedge fund manager is the beginning of a relationship that should stand the test of time and market volatility. For both the investor and the manager it is an investment in trust and character of both the parties. This trust can only be built if both the parties are willing to discuss all the issues pertaining to the investment openly and in depth. If a hedge fund manager is elusive or haughty at the onset of the relationship, it certainly does not bode well for the rigorous ongoing due diligence process that I have laid out in my earlier chapters. When I started in the industry, I was advised by an industry colleague to water down my strategy description because the fund of funds I was meeting with would not understand much of it any way. It is true and very shameful that the lack of expertise in the fund of funds industry and the ridiculous due diligence process has frustrated a lot of hedge fund managers. This breakdown of communication channels is one of the biggest culprits in spawning scam artists because it lets the charlatans hide behind the façade of reputation, secrecy, and exclusivity. The fund of funds industry needs to start acting like bosses and asking pertinent questions, which will not only limit the scams but also win the respect of the hedge fund managers.

Often times a hedge fund manager will send his CEO, risk manager, or other senior traders to due diligence meetings with investors, as the demands of managing the portfolio can be quite time consuming and should always be the manager's first priority. While it is not imperative that the hedge fund manager show up to every single due diligence meeting, he should be well represented and should be met with at least once before the onset of the investment.

STRATEGY-RELATED QUESTIONS

The strategy level questions should still continue to cover all the basic information, including the geography, asset classes, and instruments traded. Geography and asset classes do not provide diversification, but it is important to know if the hedge fund manager's experience matches his trading mandate. After these basics are covered, we need to get into the trading methodologies to determine if the strategy is truly an alpha strategy or if it can be duplicated easily through a beta approach. As I have discussed earlier, trading methodologies will fall into one of the four categories or a combination of them:

1. Mean Reversion
2. Positive Carry
3. Systematic or High Frequency
4. Momentum

When I presented the above hypothesis to my friend, Jamie, he remarked that I was missing a bucket because I did not have a bucket for his pure arbitrage strategy. Following is an excerpt of our conversation:

Me: Jamie, how does your strategy work?

Jamie: In the credit markets we can find cases where the sum of the components of an index does not always equal the index. Therefore, by buying the index and selling a basket of the individual components I can capture pure arbitrage returns.

Me: Ok, but let me ask you a question. How did the basket get misaligned in the first place and does this happen often or infrequently?

Jamie: Well, you know, markets are not efficient. (I can feel the frown of the Chicago academia). Due to constant supply and demand imbalances or short-term volatility the index gets misaligned. But it always reverts back to its true valuation, or if I just hold the basket to maturity it settles to the same value as the index.

Me: Jamie, you just answered your own question. The perfect bucket for your strategy is mean reversion. In your case, the basket got misaligned due to a volatility shock, and as volatility subsides the basket reverts to its mean, which in your case is a certain mathematical value.

Therefore, it is important to ascertain not only the bucket that the trading methodology belongs to, but also how it reacts to rising and falling volatility as well volatility shocks; the breakdown of returns between carry and capital gains and position duration. All these factors help in determining the correlation of the strategy to a fund of funds' existing portfolio. If a hedge fund manager employs multiple methodologies, for example, mean reversion and momentum, which a lot of global macro managers do, then the fund of funds needs to track the distribution between the buckets as part of the ongoing due diligence to maintain diversity in his portfolio. As a side note, if a hedge fund manager tells you that he trades all of the above-mentioned methodologies and is well diversified across the entire spectrum of risk and return characteristics, then either you are speaking with a true multi-strategy hedge fund or a noncompliant manager. Either way, a fund of funds has no business investing in either. A true multi-strategy hedge fund should already provide the benefits of diversification and has enough visibility that it should be approached directly by the end investors (pension funds, family offices, etc.) and their consultants. There is nothing proprietary about revealing information on trading methodology. Therefore, a noncompliant manager is either not knowledgeable enough about his own strategy, a charlatan like Bernie Madoff, or just simply put, a pain in the ass to deal with. Steer clear of all of the above.

The next step is to get more information on the underlying markets. Because the new fund of funds model will have trading managers with market expertise, they should have a very good idea of the market sophistication in terms of liquidity, events risks, shorting capabilities, as well as other peculiarities. Here is a potential exchange with a global macro hedge fund manager, Steve, on the emerging markets of Asia Pacific:

Investor: Steve, you said that you will trade the emerging markets of Asia Pacific. In which countries and asset classes are you planning on concentrating?

Steve: We will concentrate on China, India, and the other South East Asian countries.

Investor: And you will trade the currency, equity, and bond markets there?

Steve: Yes.

Investor: What instruments are available to you for shorting these markets? As I understand, the governments in India and China do not allow shorting of the stock markets.

Steve: Shorting the currencies is clearly not a problem. As for interest rates, we can take a short view through the interest rate swaps market. Equities will be a problem. But we plan to use Total Return Swaps with some onshore counterparties for expressing our short view in equities.

Investor: Before we get into equities, let us talk about the shorting of rates. Most Asian countries have a two-tier market, one for the onshore participants and one for the offshore. I presume you will participate in the offshore market? What about the fixing and the basis risk?

Steve: The fixing rate for all payments is set by the market participants but we do run a risk on the basis between the onshore and the offshore markets.

Investor: Steve, on the equities it sounds like you will have mostly a long-only strategy with ad-hoc shorting capabilities?

Steve: Yes, for all intents and purposes we plan to generate alpha by either being long or flat in the equities.

Investor: Presumably you could take a cross asset short position as well through the currency markets.

Steve: Yes, but the correlation is not too good.

Investor: I am worried that I will be paying alpha fees on the equity part of the portfolio for what could turn out to be just market beta returns.

Steve: Uhhh . . . but we will be trading other asset classes as well.

Investor: How do you plan to handle gap risks arising from political instability and government interventionist policies?

Steve:	Well, first, our momentum-based methodology requires us to take short-term positions. Second, we also plan on using options to express a lot of our views, which by default buys us protection against unforeseen market developments as well.
Investor:	Good, I think it is very important to have a few small positions with short holding periods rather than to get married to one or two large positions in emerging markets.
Investor:	Given your underlying markets, the capacity of your fund should be limited, correct?
Steve:	Yes. To keep the position sizing manageable and to keep the fund nimble, we plan on closing around $1 billion.

The above sample exchange between a hedge fund investor and the hedge fund manager is a dialogue. Both parties are knowledgeable about the markets and are capable of engaging in an in-depth discussion on the risks and opportunities involved with an investment in the global macro momentum trading space in the emerging markets of Asia. After a meeting such as this, the investor walks away feeling a lot more confident in the manager's abilities, and the manager knows that he will be working with an investor who will base his decisions on rational and information-driven processes rather than on greed and fear.

WHAT QUALIFIES YOU TO EXECUTE THIS STRATEGY?

Once the investor has obtained enough information on the strategy and the underlying markets to become comfortable with the investment's ability to generate alpha and how it will fit into the existing portfolio, the next step is to ensure that the hedge fund manager possesses the necessary skills to execute the strategy.

The due diligence should start with the manager's educational background. A doctor who has not attended a medical college or a pilot who has not attended flight school would raise red flags. Similarly, a hedge fund manager who claims to have, for example, a high-frequency systematic trading strategy with no requisite training in mathematics, quantitative finance, or sciences should raise a red flag as well. While it is true that quite a few strategies such as long-short equity, momentum, macro, etc., do not require specific training, quite a few other more esoteric strategies do. A hedge fund manager like Bernie Madoff, whose entire strategy was based on expressing his views through derivative instruments, should have a good grasp of options theory and calculus. A high-frequency trader should be able to discuss his models and the basic principles guiding them, such as pattern recognition algorithms, neural networks, and other models.

When I used to interview traders for my desk, I would always look for a world-class university on the resume. There is a certain amount of comfort in knowing that a certain level of due diligence has already been performed on the manager by a world-class academic institution. The process of applying to, getting accepted into, and graduating from a world-class university acts as a natural filter that separates the brightest and the most ambitious from the rest. Just as I would want the best-educated doctor looking after my health, I would want the best-educated hedge fund manager looking after my wealth. Below is a list of the top U.S. and non U.S.–based MBA programs as ranked by *BusinessWeek* magazine for 2008. The list below is not exhaustive by any means for judging a hedge fund manager's academic credentials. Quite a few strategies that are very quantitative in nature would require Masters degrees and PhDs in technical fields, and institutions such as CalTech, IIT (Indian Institute of Technology), while not listed below, would be a part of such a list.

Top 10 U.S. Programs

1. University of Chicago (Booth)
2. Harvard University
3. Northwestern University (Kellogg)
4. University of Pennsylvania (Wharton)
5. University of Michigan (Ross)
6. Stanford University
7. Columbia University
8. Duke University (Fuqua)
9. MIT (Sloan)
10. UC Berkeley (Haas)

Top 10 Non-U.S. MBA Programs

1. Queen's University, Canada
2. IE Business School, Spain
3. INSEAD, France
4. Western Ontario (Ivey), Canada
5. London Business School, UK
6. ESADE, Spain
7. IMD, Switzerland
8. Toronto (Rotman), Canada
9. IESE, Spain
10. Oxford (Saîd), UK

WORK EXPERIENCE

Once the hedge fund manager's academic credentials have been established, the fund of funds needs to ensure that the hedge fund manager has experience trading that strategy and will not be experimenting with your capital and at your expense. In Chapter 3, I showed the career path of a trader and how he develops his skills trading on a proprietary desk of a Wall Street bank. It is here that he makes his mistakes, gets guidance from a rabbi, develops his own unique style of trading, and matures from a caterpillar to a butterfly. Here is a potential due diligence dialogue with a hedge fund manager, Bernie:

Investor:	Bernie, you said your strategy is called split strike convergence. Can you explain the construction in greater detail?
Bernie:	The strategy involves buying the index, selling calls to give up some of the potential upside gains, and buying puts to protect against the potential losses on the long index position
Investor:	Hmmm . . . and are the calls and puts a net zero cost transaction?
Bernie:	Yes, I am striking the puts and calls about the same distance from the index price to offset the put purchase with the call sale.
Investor:	So, in essence you are always long the market, and this is a risk-defined bullish equity strategy. Tell me, how many years have you traded this strategy and how has it done in a bear market?
Bernie:	Well, I have successfully run a major brokerage operation for several years and I am the Chairman of the NASDAQ. That more than qualifies me to run this strategy.
Investor:	So, you are telling us that you have never traded this strategy. What makes you think it will work? How does being a broker qualify you to become a hedge fund trader? Have you hired qualified traders to execute this strategy for you? Can we talk to them instead?
Bernie:	Yes, I have several traders working for me, but no you cannot talk to them as this strategy is very secret.
Investor:	Bernie, so far we have not seen anything remotely secret about your strategy. Because you cannot explain your strategy and you will not let us talk to your traders, we cannot invest. Thanks for your time.

Here is a second sample exchange with a global macro trader, Warren.

Investor:	Warren, can you please outline your experience as a global macro trader?
Warren:	I have traded the global macro markets for the past ten years. I concentrate on the G7 space specifically. I spent two years as a junior trader at Bank Big Capital before being promoted to a senior trader where I had my own capital and track record. Then I joined Bank Bigger Capital as a head trader and executed my strategy along with managing a desk of seven other traders.
Investor:	And you have a track record from those years that we can verify?
Warren:	Yes.
Investor:	Warren, global macro space in the G7 markets is a very crowded space. What is your edge in this space, what makes you better than the others?
Warren:	It is my understanding of the fiat money principles. I feel that most of the market participants analyze soft currency economics from a fixed currency perspective and draw incorrect conclusions. I have actually written a book explaining the principles of fiat money.
Investor:	Impressive. Maybe we should read that book as well. Okay, now let us discuss some trade examples. Take us through a couple of trades that you executed in the past that worked well and a couple that did not. I want to hear about the analysis and thinking behind the trades, how they were executed, risk managed, and closed out. Then we can discuss some of your current views on the market and why you feel that they are right.

The second discussion clearly shows a hedge fund manager who has a lot of experience trading his strategy, a clear edge against his peers, and a track record to back his claims as well. By going through the trade examples, the investor will be able to learn a lot about how the hedge fund manager thinks. By listening to the manager's market views the fund of funds expert can compare those with his own and can engage in a healthy debate to further test the manager.

RISK APPETITE

There is an old saying that everybody has heard of, but it has never rung more true than it does for traders—"No Risk, No Reward." Having a healthy risk appetite is a critical requirement for any hedge fund trader. After all, the reason why we invest in hedge funds is because we want higher returns while acknowledging that we are taking higher risks as well. And that is the reason why we pay a 2 and 20 fee structure to the hedge fund manager. If we wanted to play it safe, we would buy government treasury bonds and clip coupons. A hedge fund manager with a low-risk appetite will not only miss out on profitable opportunities, but he will become content to collect the 2 percent annuity in management fees for sitting on your capital. This, in fact, is becoming a big problem with the hedge fund managers as well as the fund of funds and is a manifestation of the skewed compensation structure due to fixed management fees.

When I was running a trading desk for BNP Paribas in Singapore, I had a trader, Joe, who understood the Australian interest rate market incredibly well. He had traded that market for over 15 years and knew the source of the flows and the market participants very well. One day Joe came to me and took me through a trade idea. He stepped me through the analysis of the market flows, market technicals, as well as the upcoming RBA (Reserve Bank of Australia) monetary policy statement that would act as an impetus for the trade performance. I was completely convinced in the trade and told him to execute the trade in a decent size for his portfolio. I also decided to execute some of it in my own portfolio as well. The RBA announcement led to the predicted market movement and the trade started performing very well. I turned around to congratulate Joe, who used to sit right behind me, on his analysis but saw that he was acting quite sheepish. He proceeded to tell me that he backed out of the trade as he was not completely convinced that the timing was quite right, and he was waiting for a better entry point. There was nothing wrong with the timing; Joe simply developed cold feet. In the trading world there is another saying, "A lost trade opportunity is worse than a trade that has gone bad."

Here are some of the questions I would ask this trader Joe, to determine his risk appetite:

Investor: Joe, how do you handle volatile markets? Do you tend to wait till the dust settles or do you like to jump in?

Joe would most likely answer that he would wait till the dust settled before he jumped in. But the reality is that volatility creates opportunities, unless you are a carry trader who likes to collect pennies in front of the steamroller. Most traders look forward to volatile markets because they create dislocations and price movements that can be captured with good analysis and strong risk management. Volatile markets do not make for a peaceful night's sleep, but then again trading and the world of hedge fund investing is not for the faint of heart. You want your hedge fund manager to thrive in volatility markets.

Investor:	Joe, after a string of bad trades, how do you handle the next set of trades?
Joe:	After a string of bad trades, I like to cut down the position size of my next set of trades and tighten my stop loss limits until I start winning on trades again.

This is the classic response of a trader whose risk appetite will get dampened if he hits a slump. There is no correlation between the position sizing and stop loss limits of the losing trades and the new trades. Joe should instead try to determine the reasons why his previous trades went bad and concentrate on better analysis. If he is convinced in his analysis, the trade sizing and stop loss limits should be a function of the new trade's dynamics and his portfolio size and not be affected by the previous string of losing trades. If Joe sizes his trades based on the performance of the previous trades, he will get into a cycle of putting on smaller and smaller bets on potential winners and larger and larger bets on potential losers. A recipe for underperformance.

THINKER, ADAPTER, ENTREPRENEUR?

Leaving the relative comfort of working for a large institution and starting your own hedge fund is to a certain extent a leap of faith. When a trader is working on a proprietary trading desk of a large institution, he has to only worry about portfolio management. All the headaches of managing a company and its employees and dealing with government regulations, etc., are handled by a large army of middle and back office professionals. At a hedge fund, the manager wears several hats. Usually, the manager will retain portfolio responsibilities as the Chief Investment Officer while delegating the role of running the company to other people. But the hedge fund manager is the majority shareholder in his management company and therefore wedded to the administration of the company as well. The manager would be consulted on and involved in the resolution of any unforeseen hurdles that the company might encounter. Therefore, the hedge fund manager needs to be versatile, able to adapt to non-market-related challenges and changes, and think like an entrepreneur. These qualities are not imbued overnight and some streaks of them should be evident in the manager's past. Here are some of the questions I would ask hedge fund manager Simon, to determine if he has shown entrepreneurialism in his past:

Investor:	Simon, I am sure you realize the challenges of running a company while managing a portfolio as well are quite unique. What makes you think you will succeed?
Simon:	Yes, I am quite aware of the increased responsibilities. I have hired a Chief Executive Officer as well as a Chief Operations Officer to handle most of those responsibilities.
Investor:	But you must retain the majority of the financial interest in the company, right? You can't tell me that you will be happy giving up all executive control of your company to a couple of employees. I know I would not.
Simon:	Yes I do retain 90 percent of the financial interest in my company. I am the president of the board as well so will be presiding over all executive committee meetings. But I thrive on increased challenges, and one of my passions has always been in trying to build a business. I ran a small business on the weekends while I was attending college. I left a secure job to accept responsibility for building a new business at a new bank and now again I left a secure job to start a hedge fund.

Simon clearly has a streak of passion for running businesses. His motivation for starting his hedge fund is not just the allure of increased compensation but the thrill of being his own boss and creating a company in his own image. He will need this enthusiasm as he encounters unforeseen problems. He will have to adapt, to overcome apparently insurmountable obstacles, and if he does succeed, he will end up creating another hedge fund industry giant like a Millennium or Tudor. But the reality is that less than one-third of the hedge funds survive after the first three years, and a lot of them fail due to business and operational issues rather than poor performance.

DISCIPLINE AND CHARACTER

No amounts of academic credentials, trading experience, risk appetite, or entrepreneurialism can make up for a lack of discipline and poor character. The best-laid risk management plans will fail if they are not followed. When a trader is making money and is feeling confident, it is much easier for him, from an emotional perspective, to stick to his trading discipline. But when he starts losing money, starts nearing his stop loss levels, and starts to get worried about his job or the survival of his fund, his true character reveals itself. Most traders at one point in their career have either inflated their profits by marking their books egregiously or let their stop loss discipline slide a bit. Most of these traders had good character and ended up correcting their mistakes, some did not and got caught, and some are still out there wrestling with their conscience and trying to sweep the ever-mounting losses under the rug.

As a fund of funds investor, the single most crucial piece of due diligence that needs to be done is on the fund manager's discipline and character. Often this bit of due diligence is mistaken for just checking a trader's background, talking to his references, and checking for any action by the regulatory agencies. This is clearly insufficient. When a trader inflates his profits or racks up massive losses by failing to follow his due diligence, his infractions rarely are reported to any outside agency. Unless the infraction is of catastrophic levels, a bank or hedge fund will quietly strike a deal with the trader. They will both part company and the entire incident gets swept under the rug. A trader has enough contacts and friends in the industry, which is a very small and exclusive club, that he can always get glowing recommendations. Therefore, the best tool a fund of funds investor has to check a trader's discipline and character is the initial interview process and strict ongoing due diligence of the trader's process. Here are some of the questions I would ask hedge fund manager Nick to delve into his discipline and character:

Investor:　Nick, I know very well about the pressures of trading, the temptations of letting your stop-loss discipline slide a bit in the hope that the position will reverse itself. I know because I am guilty of such infractions myself on more than one occasion. Have you ever come across a similar situation and how did you handle it?

Nick:　No, never. I have always followed my risk management discipline diligently.

I would not expect Nick to say anything else. Therefore, a direct approach is not the best course of action. Be cunning. Ask about the periods in Nick's trading career when he was down. Check the months, quarters, and years when he lost money and see how those losses compared to his stop-loss levels. If Nick replies that he has never had a significant down period, then one of the following is true:

■ Nick is a phenomenal trader and you should invest with him.
■ Nick does not have a long enough trading history.
■ Nick is lying.

Most likely, choices two or three are true and Nick's response should tell you something about Nick's character as well.

Investor: Nick, tell me about 2008. I see that you finished the year down 15 percent. How did that compare to your annual drawdown limit?

Nick: My annual drawdown limit was 15 percent. I was doing fine until about October of 2008 when I incurred all the losses.

At this point, the investor should delve more into the positions that caused the massive losses in the fourth quarter of 2008 and see how they tally with the market movements in that quarter. I would be worried that Nick tried to hide the losses during the first three quarters of the year and then when he knew that the year was lost, he let them all out before the year was finished and the bank's or hedge fund's year-end accounting took place. Maybe there was nothing as insidious as that and maybe Nick did have a string of bad trades in the fourth quarter.

Investor: Nick, what about your monthly and position stop losses? It seems strange that after surviving a difficult year you would suddenly incur such steep losses over such a short period of time.

Usually, a smart trader would have hierarchical stop losses that were much smaller than the annual stop losses to prevent racking up huge losses in a short period of time. It would be worthwhile to pose such questions to Nick to determine if he did not have a monthly stop loss discipline or just decided to blow through it. But either way, a big loss over a short period of time should raise flags about discipline.

Character and discipline will reveal itself in many ways and in different facets of a person's life. Some of the questions to consider are:

1. How many times has he changed careers for parallel moves? Were these moves truly career advancements or were they just parallel moves? Maybe the trader was staying one step ahead of getting into professional problems with his old employer or maybe he lacks patience and gets bored quite easily.
2. How many times has the trader changed his trading style or trading mandates?
3. How many times has the hedge fund manager been married and divorced?

Strong character and stability go hand in hand. They let a person deal with the ups and downs in career as well as in life.

CHAPTER 11

Hedge Fund Industry's Role in 2008 Market Crisis

The 2008 stock market crash in the United States ranks as the second largest in terms of a percentage drop. From its peak of 13,930 in October 2007 to a low of 6,544 in February 2009, the Dow Jones average dropped 53 percent. This ranks as the second worst drop since the Great Depression of the 1930s, when the index dropped a whopping 89 percent. Figure 11.1 shows the Dow Jones Index prices since 1928, while Figure 11.2 shows the logarithmic values of the index, which helps in comparing the present index to its historical values.

As the stock market has taken a dive of greater than 50 percent, the employment situation has gotten worse in lock step as well. The national unemployment rate has jumped from a low of 4.4 percent in 2006 to 9.4 percent as of May 2009 and is expected to peak between 10 percent and 12 percent by the end of 2009 or early 2010, according to economists' estimates. Consequently, investors have suffered from a double whammy of a negative income effect, resulting from job losses, as well as a negative wealth effect, resulting from a drop in the value of their stock portfolios as well as the prices of their homes. As the mood of the nation's investors has turned discernibly surly, demands for inquisition into the causes of the economic downturn have been made with increased frequency and fervor. Mortgage brokers, banks, failed regulators, and even hedge funds have been blamed for causing the current market crisis. Governments across the globe have pumped trillions of dollars to shore up their banking systems and banks' day-to-day operations and business policies have come under media scrutiny like never before. Normal as well as abnormal compensation policies of failed bank executives have made headlines, resulting in widespread anger and protests. Senator Charles Schumer threatened the recipients of $165 million in bonuses at AIG, an insurance company that had to be bailed out with taxpayer dollars, with 90 percent taxes to recoup those

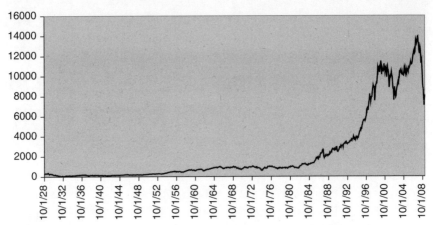

FIGURE 11.1 Dow Jones Industrial Average (1928–present monthly).

Source: Yahoo Finance

bonuses, while Senator Charles Grassley went a step ahead and asked those executives to consider committing suicide. With so much anger, allegations, and rhetoric surrounding the cause and effect of the 2008 market crisis, it is worthwhile to take a dispassionate and purely economic look at some of these causes and the involvement of hedge funds in the crisis. In the coming months and years one can expect to see reams of pages devoted to this

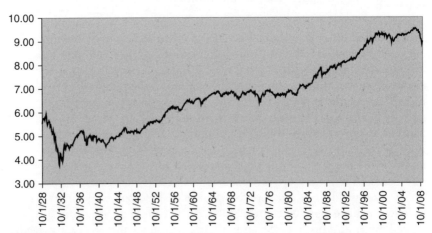

FIGURE 11.2 Dow Jones Industrial Average (1928–present monthly)—logarithmic.

Source: Yahoo Finance

subject; therefore, I will approach my discussion from a failure of due diligence as well as a regulatory oversight perspective.

BORROWERS, BANKERS, AND INVESTORS

In the simplest terms, the 2008 market crisis was caused by the proliferation of financial instruments that promoted irresponsible borrowing and thereby rampant speculation on real estate prices. Rising interest rates and defaults by the low credit borrowers caused the real estate bubble to burst, which left anybody holding these sub-prime bonds with little or no value. The flow chart in Figure 11.3 shows the various players involved in this trade, and at the end of the day all of them share in the blame for the 2008 market crisis.

The last asset bubble to burst in the United States was the Internet bubble of the late 1990s that burst in the year 2000. The corresponding monetary policy response by the Federal Reserve Bank brought the interest rates down from over 6 percent in 2000 to 1 percent by the end of 2003. A combination of a loss of faith in the stock market and low yields offered by government bonds left the investors with few options where they could earn a decent rate of return while preserving their capital. The phrase "safe as a house" was on everybody's lips as they slowly started directing their capital into the housing market. Then came the unfortunate terrorist attacks of September 11, 2001, which heightened a sense of patriotism as well as a desire to invest in assets that would promote a better lifestyle. American culture and thereby popular media has always promoted the "American Dream" of owning your own home, the proverbial four-bedroom house in the suburbs with a yard and a white picket fence. It does not take a leap of

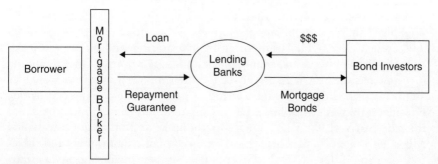

FIGURE 11.3 2008 Market crisis players.

faith to realize that all the catalysts were in place to spark a housing boom that began in earnest in 2004 and lasted well through 2006.

Initially, most of the money that went into the housing market was for primary residences and was borrowed by responsible borrowers with good credit ratings and a sustainable income stream to repay these loans. Data on housing prices show that over the long term, housing prices compound at the rate of inflation. But between 2004 and 2006, national housing prices on average increased by 30 percent while the most speculative markets like Florida went up by 60 percent. A big cause of these price increases was not the purchase of primary residences but the speculative activity as the housing industry started attracting investor capital to try to capture these 15 to 30 percent annualized gains in house prices.

DON'T BLAME THE PRODUCTS, BLAME THE USERS

Banks on Wall Street are very good at recognizing demand for certain assets and then facilitating that demand by innovating new financial products. The mortgage lending banks introduced products like ARMs (Adjustable Rate Mortgages) and their derivatives, as well as other high-interest rate mortgage products. These were marketed very aggressively and often unscrupulously by mortgage brokers to first-time home buyers, home buyers with nonverifiable or unsustainable incomes, home buyers with junk credit ratings, i.e., sub prime, and investors who were looking to simply trade, i.e., buy, hold for a few months and then sell the house to capture capital gains. For all intents and purposes these new financial products let an investor leverage his or her income and capital to purchase a more expensive home or several homes that he or she normally would not have able to afford. During 2006, 22 percent of homes purchased were for investment purposes, with an additional 14 percent purchased as vacation homes. During 2005, these figures were 28 percent and 12 percent respectively.

This flow of capital to fund the housing boom would not have been possible if there were no lenders supplying the capital. At the end of the day, every asset bubble is supported by investor demand that is willing to bear the risks in hopes of reaping quick and large rewards. Once again the investment banks on Wall Street started their financial innovation engines and transformed the mortgages, written by the lending commercial banks, into investable securities like CDOs (Collateralized Debt Obligations) and their derivatives, like CDO squared structures, and other multi-tranched MBSs (Mortgage Backed Securities) with different credit ratings and therefore offering different yields. Given a lack of investment options with attractive returns, a lot of investors were attracted to these mortgage-linked securities, some of which were offering yields as high as 10 to 12 percent. The investors in these securities included the commercial lending banks themselves, hedge funds, and individual investors, as well as pension funds of companies and other countries.

As we are and will continue to sift through the rubble of this market crisis for several years to come, it is very important to analyze the root causes of the crisis and separate perception from reality. Financial innovation and the Wall Street banks that came up with these securities have been blamed for fueling the housing boom and bust. Innovation, be it financial or technological, is at the heart of capitalism and one of the main drivers of American dominance and prosperity. It is never the product that should carry the blame, but the user who misuses it. Advances in nuclear physics have provided benefits in the field of medicine, biology, energy, and manufacturing and have led to an improvement in living standards of millions of people around the world. But they have also led to the development of weapons of mass destruction. Similarly, advances in financial technology have improved the efficiency of the real estate market by providing broader access to capital for buyers and opportunities for higher returns for investors. The key point for the regulators to consider is not to blame the technology itself or revile the innovators, but to put in place regulations to prevent the abuse of these products to prevent similar crisis in the future.

FAILED DUE DILIGENCE ON PART OF INVESTORS

When it is time to share the blame pie, a portion of it will go to the investors into mortgage-linked securities who failed to recognize the risks associated with these securities and kept supplying the market with ever-increasing amounts of capital. A large portion of blame will also go to the mortgage brokers for not executing the responsibility of vetting the borrowers that they were entrusted with, and the remainder of the blame will lie with the borrowers themselves who flat out lied on their mortgage applications, which is a criminal offense in itself.

The investors who purchased these mortgage-linked securities have no one to blame but themselves for their incompetent due diligence as well as a breakdown of their internal risk management systems. Retail investors, like wealthy individuals, and institutional investors, like banks and hedge funds, that purchased these mortgage-linked securities failed to realize the risks embedded in the securities—they were solely enamored by the high returns. Investment banks like Bear Stearns, Lehman Brothers, Merrill Lynch, and investment arms of insurers like AIG failed at their responsibility of determining the risks involved with these products. The same applies to the commercial lending banks like Wells Fargo and Citibank who issued these securities and invested in them as well. According to HFN Hedge Fund Industry Report, hedge fund asset inflows increased over 100 percent and went from $1.4 trillion at the end of 2004 to nearly $3 trillion by the middle of 2008. A lot of this hedge fund capital inflow was directed at credit strategy hedge funds that invested in the mortgage backed securities as well. If these investors had conducted proper risk assessment of the mortgage securities and realized the risks embedded in them, they would have curtailed the amount of capital that would have flowed into the housing market. A lack of capital flow would have automatically checked the speculative activity in the real estate market, and capitalism would have acted as its own regulator.

No amount of government-imposed regulation can ever make up for complete and, more important, proper due diligence that needs to be conducted by investors. The single most important regulation that the government can stipulate is that all investment products offer complete transparency. Be it MBSs, CDOs, or credit strategy hedge funds, it is important to know the true makeup of the investment product. Retail investors need to hire experts who can understand the risks in these investments, and institutional investors need to ensure that they have the requisite staff that can understand and properly evaluate the investment decisions (subject of much discussion in earlier chapters). At the end of the day, it is not some government entity, but an educated and diligent investor, who will be the best regulator of the capital markets.

FAILURE OF FIDUCIARY RESPONSIBILITIES BY BROKERS AND LIES BY BORROWERS

A large part of the blame for the current market crisis also lies with the abuse of these products, like the ARMs and sub-prime mortgages, by the mortgage brokers who sold them aggressively, and the borrowers who blatantly provided false data about their incomes. The mortgage brokers were solely interested in making as many loans as they could, as their compensation was directly tied to the volume of loans underwritten. They had no incentive to verify the veracity of the data provided by the borrowers. Similarly, a lot of the borrowers were enticed by the fact that they could borrow large sums of money to buy "the house of their dreams," irrespective of their ability to repay the loan. Some borrowers were just short-term investors, who relied on house prices to continue rising and whose intention was to flip the house a few months later for a tidy profit.

This is an area where government regulation needs to be strengthened. Mortgage brokers need to be held to the same standard as securities brokers. Currently, there are no uniform standards for mortgage brokers; the rules and laws vary by state. The states differ on whether a mortgage broker even needs a mortgage license, whether the mortgage broker can loan on both first and second mortgages, or whether a physical office in the state is required. As business over the Internet increases, the mortgage licensing laws are becoming more lenient on the physical office requirement. States also differ on how much continuing education is required for the mortgage broker to continue practicing. Moreover, most states' mortgage licensing laws only cover the company and few require licenses for the employees of the mortgage broker company. The regulators need to come up with a uniform set of rules that must apply across the industry for the registration and education of mortgage brokers. Furthermore, rules on disclosure of risks involved in various structured mortgage loans should be strengthened, and finally, the mortgage broker's compensation needs to be tied to the performance of the loan to align the interests of the loan originator and the loan investor.

Besides the investors and the mortgage brokers, the final part of the blame must lie with the mortgage borrowers who lied on their applications and therefore should be prosecuted to prevent a repeat of such occurrences in the future. Unfortunately, the policies coming out of Washington are very short-sighted in nature and politically driven, which will end up rewarding poor investment decision making by investors, short-term business decision making by banks, and greed and lying by the borrowers. Why? Because they know that they will be bailed out with economic stimulus bills, mortgage relief plans, TARPs, and TALFs of the future. The only way to drastically reduce the chances of the next market crisis is to adopt a Darwinian approach, which will ensure that the lessons from the current crisis are not forgotten with the inflating of the next asset bubble.

NO HEDGE FUND HAS BEEN BAILED OUT

On November 13, 2008, a congressional committee grilled five of the top hedge fund managers in the world about the role of the hedge fund industry in the current market crisis. These five included John Paulson, James Simons, Philip Falcone, George Soros, and Ken Griffin. The hedge fund industry has been accused of creating excessive market volatility, carrying large undisclosed risks, market manipulation while short selling bank stocks, and possibly creating systemic risk due to their size.

Every single hedge fund manager present at the hearing echoed the same sentiment: that hedge funds were not to blame for the financial crisis that wreaked havoc on Wall Street as well as Main Street. They touted the hedge fund industry as a source of capital that will eventually help in restoring liquidity and stability to the financial markets. Furthermore, the market did not see a repeat of 1998, when the hedge fund, Long Term Capital Management, had to be rescued by a consortium of banks that was facilitated by the Federal Reserve Bank of New York.

Hedge funds, however, are not completely disconnected from the crisis. They have been blamed for violating short-selling rules and rumor mongering, as well as creating systemic risk due to their derivatives portfolios. Hedge funds have been hurt by the crisis as well; some have lost trading counterparties that ended up being merged with other banks, like Merrill Lynch and Bear Stearns; some lost assets that were tied up with failed banks, like Lehman Brothers; while others had their credit lines severely reduced, resulting in forced position liquidations.

On September 22, 2008, the SEC identified six institutions, including Bear Stearns and Lehman Brothers, that might have been a target of manipulation by the short sellers. The SEC sent subpoenas to more than fifty hedge funds looking at whether they were spreading rumors about Lehman Brothers, including apparently false information about takeover talks and the possibility of government financing while short-selling their stocks. In a regular short sale, a trader sells borrowed stock in hopes that it drops and can be bought at a lower price. Under SEC rules, a trader needs to locate stock to borrow ahead of a short sale, and the stock needs to be delivered within three trading days. The SEC, as well as the management of Lehman Brothers and Bear Stearns, felt that rules were broken when the short sellers did not borrow stock to cover their short positions. This resulted in the short-sale volume being larger than the total amount of stock outstanding, resulting in artificial pressure on the stock price and thereby forcing bankruptcy of the companies.

This is clearly an area where the SEC needs to strengthen and enforce regulation. Capital markets will self-govern effectively as long as the rules of the game are being applied uniformly and followed diligently. Short selling itself is not to blame; it is a very important tool for the proper functioning of capital markets. Short selling ensures that stock prices do not get overheated and provides a natural balance for the marketplace, a bull and a bear. However, as stated earlier, it is not the instrument but the user that has to take the blame for the misuse. If a short seller violates the SEC rules and does not cover his position by borrowing outstanding stock in the market, he changes the rules of the game by artificially creating downward pressure on the stock price. SEC regulation needs to enforce the short covering rule to even the playing field.

On September 18, 2008, New York Attorney General Andrew Cuomo announced that he was launching a "wide-ranging" investigation into short selling. His aim is to prosecute any short sellers engaging in any improper conduct, including, but not limited to, the spreading of false rumors. One of Mr. Cuomo's objectives is to stabilize the markets by "rooting out short sellers who spread false information." Unfortunately, rumor mongering has always been a part and parcel of free democratic markets and will be much harder to stamp out.

SYSTEMIC RISK AND DERIVATIVE TRANSACTIONS

There has also been a lot of talk lately about regulating OTC or non-exchange traded derivative instruments. Currently, these instruments are traded between two counterparties based on mutually agreed-upon terms and conditions. Given the lack of a central platform, like an exchange, the volume of OTC derivative transactions is unknown as is the systemic risk stemming from the interconnected counterparty credit risk from these instruments. Here is an example to better understand the systemic risk inherent in OTC derivative transactions. Say Goldman Sachs trades a CDS (credit default swap) with a hedge fund. A few days later the hedge fund decides to unwind the risk on that CDS, so it does an offsetting transaction with JP Morgan. The hedge fund has no market risk at this point but has outstanding credit risk with two counterparties. The number of such derivative transactions and the resulting outstanding credit risk increases with the size of the hedge fund. In 1998, while assessing Long Term Capital Management's outstanding credit risk to the banks on Wall Street, Peter Fisher from the NY Fed calculated that the potential losses to the street could be as high as $5 billion. Long Term's assets under management at that point were around $3 billion. The largest hedge funds these days run capital in excess of $10 billion and the number of derivative transactions has only increased.

One suggestion being floated around, quite vehemently, to regulate the systemic risk involved in derivative instruments, is to standardize the terms of over-the-counter derivative instruments, such as credit default swaps, and to cause those instruments to be traded on futures or options exchanges. The arguments in favor of such a move are as follows:

- Standardization would have the benefit of reducing the opaque nature of the derivative instruments.

- The nature of the obligations owed by each party and the amounts of those obligations would be better known. The exchange and its clearing corporation would be able to monitor the risks being undertaken by each of the parties trading on the exchange and to establish limits on their positions. These limits would be designed to limit the risk of the clearing corporation as to any single trading party and would also have substantial systemic benefits.
- Exchange trading of these standard contracts would place a well-financed exchange clearing corporation as a responsible party on each of the contracts traded on the exchange, thereby eliminating the counterparty risks.

The suggestion to standardize the terms of over-the-counter derivative instruments has some valid points, especially the fact that the centralized exchange would be able to monitor the risk taken by a counterparty and limit it by stipulating margin requirements. The second valid point is that by having a centralized clearing facility, the layers of nested counterparty risks that stem from derivative transactions would be eliminated, thereby eliminating systemic risk that arises from large hedge funds. On the negative side, this argument completely misses the point of OTC transactions. The market needs specific and tailored derivative transactions, which is the reason why the OTC market came to life in the first place.

Consider a U.S. corporation that does business in Europe and thereby has a stream of cash flows in foreign currencies in the future. This corporation wisely decides not to subject its shareholders to undue currency exchange risk, so it wants to hedge out this risk. The problem is that the dates on which it is supposed to receive the cash flows might not match the standardized terms of an exchange traded transaction and would require specific terms and conditions that can be arranged only through an OTC transaction.

Another example of such a need could be from a relative value hedge fund. If the hedge fund manager realizes that there is value in shorting the 6.5-year Japanese government bonds while buying 14.5-year bonds and shorting the 22.5-year bond, and he wants to structure this transaction in an interest rate option format, it would be impossible for him to execute this transaction on an exchange with standardized terms.

Perhaps the solution to this problem is best left to the market participants who would have to revise their own internal market and credit risk systems to ensure that positions with counterparties are well collateralized and are margined frequently. It is also true that once the banks realize that there is no government bailout safety net in place, they will be more apt to be diligent with their internal risk management systems and reduce the amount of leverage they deploy.

REGULATING HEDGE FUNDS

Since the Federal Reserve Bank of New York organized the rescue of Long Term Capital Management in 1998, there has been much speculation on the risks posed by the hedge funds to the investors and the financial markets as a whole. With every economic downturn come the vociferous cries for regulating these vast unregulated and unregistered pools of investment capital, totaling nearly $1.8 trillion dollars at the start.

One of the proponents of regulation, Professor David S. Ruder, testified before the House of Representatives Committee on Oversight and Government Reform on November 13, 2008 arguing for the benefits of registering hedge funds with the SEC. His main arguments are summarized as follows:

- Registering hedge funds with the SEC will allow the SEC to inspect hedge fund books and possibly identify fraudulent activities at an earlier stage.
- Registering hedge funds will give the SEC the power to require disclosure of activities that might injure investors, power to require hedge fund advisers to disclose hedge fund risk activities, and power to monitor and assess the effectiveness of hedge fund risk management systems.
- Professor Ruder believes the Securities and Exchange Commission understands the markets and therefore is the best organization for monitoring and assessing hedge fund risk management systems to ensure that those systems are effective in meeting their protective goals.

The basic premise of Professor Ruder's argument is that the SEC possesses the necessary skilled professionals with years of hands-on market experience in the field of trading and risk management that they can effectively monitor and assess risks posed by hedge funds. In Chapter 5, I outlined how Harry Markopolos approached the SEC several times over a period of eight years raising several red flags about Bernie Madoff's operation, and after conducting its due diligence, the SEC kept giving Madoff a clean bill of health. The SEC does not understand the markets; it has no experience in esoteric hedge fund trading strategies and the risks emanating from such strategies. Therefore, it does not possess the tools or the skills required to monitor hedge fund risks. Designating the SEC as the watchdog over hedge funds will end up providing a false panacea to the investors, who might feel that they do not have to perform as much due diligence on the hedge fund manager as they used to. This will also create another layer of bureaucracy that will only end up increasing the cost of running and thereby investing in a hedge fund.

The one area where the financial regulatory bodies can add value is by mandating the five inviolable commandments I stated earlier:

1. An independent industry-recognized auditor.
2. An independent industry-recognized administrator/custodian.
3. Trade execution via independent entities, like prime brokers.
4. Fund valuations conducted independently by a third party, like an administrator.
5. Complete transparency and detailed information on the strategy with regular risk and return reporting.

By mandating the abovementioned rules and by enforcing these rules, the SEC would have taken huge steps toward ensuring that scandals are avoided and the investors are provided with all the information needed in making their own educated investment decisions. The task of assessing a hedge fund's strategy and its risk should be left to the investors and their advisors. No single risk mandate can be applied across the board to the hedge fund industry. Strategies and their implementation define risk mandate, market climate defines risk mandate, and finally an investor's risk appetite defines risk mandate. Capital markets and their educated investors will always be the best regulators of hedge funds. Hopefully, I have been able to point out the several deficiencies in the hedge fund investment process that currently exist and what the future of hedge fund investing should look like.

CHAPTER 12

The End

ROBERT ALLEN STANFORD'S PONZI SCHEME

As I have been writing this book over the last few months, we have seen a few more interesting developments take place in the hedge fund industry. Yet another scandalous Ponzi scheme has unfolded, the hedge fund industry has started showing signs of taking voluntary steps in offering more disclosure, and the stock market has sunk another 15 percent into 2009.

The Securities and Exchange Commission charged that Houston billionaire R. Allen Stanford and three of his companies committed fraud when they promised steady, double-digit returns to investors who bought $8 billion worth of his businesses' certificates of deposits. Investors were promised an "improbable and unsubstantiated high interest rate," for the last 15 years, the SEC alleged. Although the Stanford companies promised that investors' money was in liquid investments, it really invested in illiquid assets, including private equity and real estate, according to court documents. Robert Allen Stanford's Chief Investment Officer, Laura Pendergast Holt, had no financial services or securities industry experience before joining Stanford companies, and a decade later was managing $15 billion in assets and running a worldwide team of financial analysts.

This time around, the victims were not the high net worth individuals of Palm Beach taking advice from their golfing buddies, but the top golfers in the world taking financial advice from their agents. The red flags that should have come up with any serious due diligence on Robert Stanford are no different from the ones involved with the Bernie Madoff scandal.

1. Returns that were too good to be true.
2. Money managers had no relevant credentials or experience.

3. A highly regarded person used his reputation and public stature to raise capital.
4. There was no reputable auditor to vet the results.

With all the uncertainties and risks involved with investing in high-return strategies, it is a real shame that even in this day and age investors keep making some of the most avoidable mistakes. Scam artists, like Bernie Madoff and Robert Stanford, will continue to prey on the unsophisticated investors, unless the investors start to heed the three simple lessons I highlighted in the Chapter 1:

1. Relationships Do Not Trump Due Diligence.
2. Investing in Hedge Funds: Hire Experts.
3. "We Did Not Know What We Were Investing In" Is Not An Excuse.

HEDGE FUND INDUSTRY OFFERS MORE DISCLOSURE

The new funds of hedge funds model I have recommended in this book requires cooperation on the part of the hedge funds in offering increased transparency on their major positions, risks, and market views. In my introduction to the book, I had stated that some critics will say that some of the hedge funds do not offer the transparency, desired liquidity, or description of the strategy to implement the new model. The disastrous performance by the hedge fund industry in 2008 combined with the scandals that have unfolded have resulted in the hedge fund industry voluntarily moving toward offering more transparency.

The Alternative Investment Management Association (AIMA) said, on February 24, 2009, it was announcing a major new transparency initiative. "We want to dispel once and for all this misconception that the hedge fund industry is opaque and uncooperative," said Andrew Baker, Chief Executive of AIMA, in a statement. AIMA is calling on its 1,200 member firms in over forty countries to subject themselves to self-regulation before international regulators do it for them. The industry group also called for unified global standards, rather than the patchwork of national regulation.

This step by the hedge fund industry is a win-win scenario for everybody except the scam artists. At the end of the day, every legitimate hedge fund wants an educated, well-informed, and rational investor who will be driven by rational processes rather than greed and fear. An educated and competent fund of funds should relish the thought of having increased transparency and by applying the new model that I have suggested they can truly execute their fiduciary responsibilities for their investors.

SIMILAR PROBLEMS WITH THE PENSION
FUNDS, ENDOWMENTS, SWFs

The focus of my attention in this book has been the funds of hedge funds. These so called experts are a crucial conduit in the flow of capital from the end investors such as pension funds, endowments, family offices, and so on to the hedge fund managers. The one class of institutional investors that I have not discussed in this book is the SWFs (Sovereign Wealth Funds). The SWFs are state- or government-owned investment funds that invest in various financial assets, including hedge funds. The SWFs acquire assets through a government's central bank activities. Central banks around the world accumulate foreign currency reserves as a function of exports, foreign direct investments, or by direct purchases in the currency markets. The reasons for accumulating foreign currency reserves are many and complex, and I do not want to digress from the main topic of this book. Suffice to say that the SWFs have become major direct investors into hedge funds of late.

While most of these institutional investors outsource the hedge fund investing process to funds of funds, quite a few of them invest in the hedge fund strategies directly. The hedge fund allocation models that are currently being utilized by the funds of funds are also being used by these institutional investors. Thus, they suffer from the same problems and can benefit from the suggested solutions as well.

Of late, some discussions have come up about institutional investors running their own multi-strategy hedge funds. According to this suggestion, the pension funds, endowments, and SWFs would hire traders, risk managers, and support personnel across a spectrum of strategies and look to replicate a hedge fund setup in-house where that institutional investor would be the sole investor into the outfit. The benefits for doing this are that the institutional investor gets complete transparency and control over its investment as well as a lower cost structure. While these are all credible and justifiable reasons, the detriments of creating an in-house multi-strategy hedge fund outweigh the benefits.

- **Lack of core competency:** Pension funds and other institutional investors do not have any core competency in hedge fund trading strategies; therefore, they will have to re-create the wheel and hire outside experts anyway.
- **Lack of diversification:** Even if they hire traders across different trading strategies, they will still have one point of failure for risk management, operational, and other infrastructure issues.
- **Smaller alpha opportunities:** By running an in-house hedge fund, the institutional investor can never capture all the alpha opportunities

available in the marketplace. It will never be able to hire traders that can replicate the success of a Steve Cohen or Jim Simons or the several other hedge funds out there that have found a niche and an alpha generation capability.

Perhaps the better alternative for the institutional investor is to run its own fund of funds based on the model described in this book. As mentioned earlier, the institutional investors are the most influential investors into hedge funds because of their size as well as their reputation as stable long-term investors. The hedge fund managers strive to get enough capital and track record under their belt before they start to seek out these institutional investors to become direct investors into their hedge funds. By creating their own fund of funds, the institutional investors can use their size and clout to negotiate the required transparency as well as better investment terms than a fund of funds can. Even though they will incur their own set of costs in running this in-house fund of funds, these costs will more than likely be lower than the fixed percentage-based fee structure of a fund of funds. By taking the lead and implementing a model that is driven by rational and informed processes rather than greed and fear, the institutional investor can directly ensure that alpha generation opportunities in the hedge fund industry continue to thrive and are not destroyed by the existing fund of funds model. After all, it is these excess market returns that the institutional investors desperately need to fulfill their own obligations as well.

The new model of hedge fund investing I have suggested in this book may not be perfect, but it certainly is much better than the existing model. I would like to end the book by a quote from James Madison's contributions to the Federalist Papers, 1787–1788, while arguing for the ratification of the Constitution:

> *It is a matter both of wonder and regret that those who raise so many objections against the new Constitution should never call to mind the defects of that which is to be exchanged for it. It is not necessary that the former should be perfect: It is sufficient that the latter is more imperfect.*

Bibliography

Chapter 1   Recent Hedge Fund Scandals

"Amaranth hedge fund losses." Econbrowser, September 29, 2006,

Burton, Katherine. "Madoff investors paid fees to funds for profits that vanished." Bloomberg News. January 9, 2009; www.bloomberg.com/apps/news?pid=news archive&sid=amj8XcwuSr0s.

Burton, Katherine, and Jenny Strasburg. December 6, 2006. "Amaranth's slide began with offer to keep star trader." Bloomberg.com.

Creswell, Julie. August 14, 2005. "Paradise and money lost." *New York Times*.

Curran, Rob. 2008. "Traders say Madoff's strategy was unworkable." *Wall Street Journal* (Eastern edition) (December 24): C5.

Frank, Robert, and Tom Lauricella. 2008. " 'Uncle Bernie' and his angry clients— Madoff created air of mystery." *Wall Street Journal* (Eastern edition) (December 20): A1.

Guerrera, Francesco, Anuj Gangahar, and Deborah Brewster. 2008. "No questions asked." *Financial Times* 19 (December 19): 57.

John Kim and Yung Bae Kim sentenced. KLFinancialReceiver.com, Message from the Receiver, July 18, 2008.

"KL Financial's top traders indicted on fraud charges." Miamiherald.com, January 11, 2007.

Lattman, Peter. 2008. "The Madoff fraud case: Merkin gets questions on Madoff." *Wall Street Journal* (Eastern edition) (December 16): A20.

McCall, Matthew. "Losing the Amaranth gamble." *Investopedia*. www.investo pedia.com/articles/07/amaranth.asp.

Mollenkamp, Carrick, Cassell Bryan-Low, and Thomas Catan. 2008. "The Madoff fraud case: Fairfield Group is forced to confront its ties—firm was part of a global network that brought in client assets and then turned them over to money manager." *Wall Street Journal* (Eastern edition) (December 17): A10.

Murphy, Stephany. 2005. "Suite of illusions." *Palm Beach Daily News* (FL) (April 3).

Musgrave, Jane. 2008. "Scandal sullies Robert Jaffe as feds probe ties to Bernard Madoff." *Palm Beach Post* (Florida) (December 20).

Prada, Paulo. 2008. "In Palm Beach, investors assume worst." *Wall Street Journal* (Eastern edition) (December 15): A16.

Searcey, Dionne, and David Gauthier-Villars. 2008. "Big Madoff investor found dead—French financier in apparent suicide in New York office; fund lost $1.5 billion." *Wall Street Journal* (Eastern edition) (December 24): A1.

Stewart, James B. 2008. "Common sense: The lessons to be learned from the Madoff scandal." *Wall Street Journal* (Eastern edition) (December 31): D1.

Strasburg, Jenny. 2008. "The Madoff fraud case: Firm touted its family connections to reassure clients." *Wall Street Journal* (Eastern edition) (December 16): A20.

Zuckerman, Gregory. "The Madoff fraud case: Fees, even returns and auditor all raised flags." *Wall Street Journal* (Eastern edition) (December 13): A7.

Chapter 2   The Players

"Alternatives attract endowment dollars; nation's colleges diversify holdings to improve returns." Bloomberg News, January 21, 2004; www.boston.com/business/articles/2004/01/21/alternatives_attract_endowment_dollars?mode=PF.

"Before Congressional panel, witnesses underscore troubling trend of underfunded state and local pension plans." House Committee on Education & the Workforce Paper; August 30, 2006, Springfield, IL; http://edworkforce.house.gov.

Brazenor, Richard. 2008. "Investing like the Harvard and Yale endowment funds." Frontier Capital Management LLP (June 24); http://74.6.239.67/search/cache?ei=UTF-8&p=Investing+like+the+Harvard+and+Yale+endowment&y=Search&fr=yfp&u=www.regattaresearch.com/pdf/Investing_Like_the_Harvard_ and_Yale_Endowment_Funds.pdf&w=investing+invest+investment+harvard+yale+endowment&d=Koz4CRlMS7mC&icp=1&.intl=us.

Dellaverson, Carlo. 2007. "Goldman Sachs: Investment bank or big hedge fund?"; www.cnbc.com/id/16597366 (January 12).

"Hedge fund survey." Rothstein Kaas, 2008.

"The intergenerational transfer of public pension promises." NBER Working Paper No. 14343."Regulatory update: Hedge fund investments by insurance companies." *HedgeWeek* 6 (March 29, 2005): 17.

Stewart, F. 2007. "Pension fund investment in hedge funds." OECD Working Papers on Insurance and Private Pensions, No. 12. OECD publishing, © OECD. doi:10.1787/086456868358.

"Underfunded pensions may bite the US energy sector." *Reuters*, November 21, 2008.

Chapter 3   Hedge Funds

"Hedge funds: It's still a man's world." *BusinessWeek*, November 17, 2004.

Lahde, Andrew. 2008. Letter. *Financial Times* (October 17, 2008).

Leary, Paul. Event-driven hedge funds—strategy outline. Eurekahedge, *Hedge Fund Monthly*.

Lux, Hal. 2006. "The secret world of Jim Simons." *Institutional Investor*. Retrieved August 15, 2006 from chesler.us/resources/link/jim_simons.pdf.

Reuters. 2007. "Renaissance hedge fund: Only scientists need apply"; www.reuters
  .com/article/fundsFundsNews/idUSN2135575220070522 (May 22).
"Trader Monthly's top 100 for 2007 unveiled." April 7, 2008. Retrieved May 25,
  2008, from www. 1440 Wall Street.com.
www.guardian.co.uk/business/2008/oct/18/banking-useconomy.

Chapter 5   Hedge Fund Service Providers and Regulators

"Kidder Peabody name to vanish—venerable presence fades after 129 years." *Wall
  Street Journal*, January 18, 1995.
SEC v. Joseph S. Forte, et al., Civil Action No. 09-0063 (PD) (E.D. Pa.). U.S.
  Securities and Exchange Commission, Litigation Release No. 20847/January 8,
  2009.
SEC v. Michael Lauer and Lancer Management Group, LLC. http://www.sec.gov/
  litigation/complaints/comp18226.htm.
Van Voris, Bob, and Patricia Hurtado."Cosmo Ponzi scheme took in $370 Million,
  U.S. says." *Bloomberg News* (January 27, 2009).
Zuckerman, Gregory, and Kara Scannell. 2008. "Madoff misled SEC in '06, got
  off." *Wall Street Journal* (December 18).

Chapter 6   Funds of Hedge Funds

Anonymous. 2009. "The Madoff fraud case: Clients sue Tremont, Argus." *Wall
  Street Journal* (Eastern edition) (January 23): C4.
Guerrera, Francesco, Anuj Gangahar, and Deborah Brewster. 2008. "No questions
  asked." *Wall Street Journal* (December 19).
Strasburg, Jenny. 2008. "MassMutual burned by Madoff—even investors in the insurance giant's Tremont Unit weren't immune." *Wall Street Journal* (Eastern
  edition) (December 22): C1.
www.fggus.com.
www.tremont.com.

Chapter 7   An Expert Failure

Davis, Ann. 2006. "Private money: The new financial order." *Wall Street Journal*
  (Eastern edition) (September 19): A1.
Davis, Ann. 2006. "Up in summer, Brian Hunter lost $5 billion in a week as market
  turned on him; a low-profile life in Calgary." *Wall Street Journal* (Eastern
  edition) (September 19): A1.
Davis, Ann. 2006. "Blue flameout: How giant bets on natural gas sank brash hedge-
  fund trader." *Wall Street Journal* (Eastern edition) (September 19): A1.
Halpern, Nimrod. "Boaz Weinstein's bad gambles in credit trading cost Deutsche
  Bank $1.8 billion in losses in 2008." *Wall Street Journal*. (February 9, 2009).

Talley, Ian. 2007. "Why ex-trader at Amaranth is crying foul." *Wall Street Journal*. (Eastern edition) (August 8): C3.

Chapter 11   Hedge Fund Industry's Role in 2008 Market Crisis

BBC. 2009. "The downturn in facts and figures." November 21, 2007. Retrieved February 18, 2009, from http://news.bbc.co.uk/2/hi/business/7073131.stm.
Center For Responsible Lending. November 27, 2007. "A snapshot of the subprime market." Retrieved March 23, 2009 from http://www.responsiblelending.org/issues/mortgage/quick-references/a-snapshot-of-the-subprime.html.
Gibson, Dunn & Crutcher LLP Publications. September 26, 2008. "Financial markets crisis: Issues for hedge funds and private equity funds."
"Grassley backtracks on AIG suicide comments." *Reuters*, March 17, 2009.
Scannell, Kara. 2008. "The financial crisis: SEC presses hedge funds." *Wall Street Journal* (Eastern edition) (September 25): A6.
"Sen. Charles Schumer threatens to recover AIG bonuses by taxation." *Los Angeles Times*, March 17, 2009.
Strasburg, Jenny. 2008. Crisis on Wall Street: Capitol Hill questions hedge-fund managers. *Wall Street Journal* (Eastern edition) (November 14): C2.
"Who wrecked the economy?" *MotherJones* June 1, 2008. Retrieved April 5, 2009, from http://www.motherjones.com/politics/2008/05/foreclosure-phil.
www.mortgagenewsdaily.com/mortgage_license/.
www.newyorkfed.org.
www.zillow.com.

Chapter 12   The End

Schaap, Paula. 2009. "Hedge fund body supports full disclosure." Hedgefund.Net (February 24).

Index